Great Exits

T H E 4 0 1

Great Exits

T H E   4 0 1

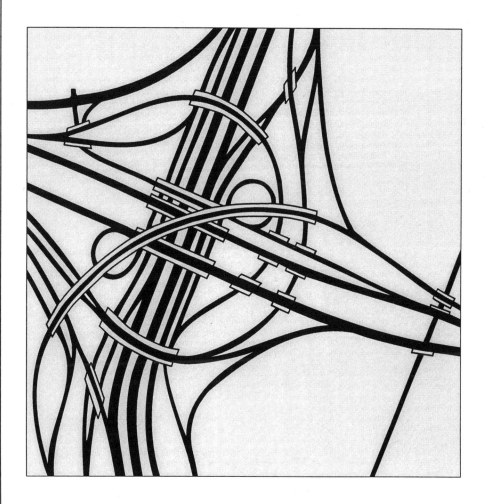

Yvonne Butorac

Stoddart

A Boston Mills Press Book

To Mike, for his infinite patience and support.

Canadian Cataloguing in Publication Data

Butorac, Yvonne, 1943–

    Great exits : the 401

ISBN 1-55046-137-0

1. Highway 401 (Ont.). 2. Highway bypasses - Ontario - Guidebooks. 3. Automobile travel - Ontario - Guidebooks. 4. Ontario - Guidebooks. I. Butorac, Mike. II. Title

GV1025.C2B8 1995   917.13   C95-930788-5

Cover and title page map graphic based on a drawing from a 1963 Ministry of Transportation report. Used with permission.

Maps by Mike Butorac
Design by Mary Firth
Printed in Canada

The publisher gratefully acknowledges the support of the Canada Council, Ontario Arts Council and Ontario Publishing Centre in the development of writing and publishing in Canada.

First published in 1995 by
The Boston Mills Press
132 Main Street
Erin, Ontario
N0B 1T0
519-833-2407   fax 833-2195

An affiliate of
Stoddart Publishing Co. Ltd.
34 Lesmill Road
North York, Ontario
M3B 2T6

Contents

Introduction

It has happened to all of us. In search of gasoline or sustenance beyond fast food, we've left Highway 401 to discover after 10 minutes of driving that we've chosen the only exit within 20 kilometres that provides a wandering tour of rural Ontario. The next time the urge to explore hits us, we quash it and safely exit at a freeway service centre.

What *does* lie beyond the next exit sign? Few of us know, and most are unwilling to risk the time to investigate. Instead, we hurtle along Ontario's main street, oblivious to small-town hospitality and perfect picnic spots.

Highway 401 was built to provide an efficient and fast road system across the province. Motorists can leave Toronto and arrive in Montreal in half a day. Goods speed from manufacturer to consumer. Commuters commute farther and faster. And yet, most of us have a love-hate relationship with the 401. Anyone who can remember the former transprovincial route, the slow and tortuous Highway 2, with a stop at every town cenotaph in its path, loves the uninterrupted speed of Highway 401. But we hate the snarled traffic; we hate the blowing snow; and most of all we hate the mesmerizing sameness. However, once we are out on the freeway and bent on reaching our destination, we rarely exit at random.

For years I missed bargains as I drove past Kingston's Division Street interchange, unaware of the factory outlet just a stone's throw away. And only recently on my regular trips to Eastern Ontario have I stopped for a picnic lunch beside Lock 2 of the Trent Canal. In almost 30 years of driving that stretch of road, I have finally taken the time to explore.

With this book, I offer you similar explorations. Take *Great Exits* along on your next Highway 401 journey. *Great Exits* describes the available services and possible diversions for each interchange from the beginning of the freeway south of Windsor to the Quebec border, 820 kilometres to the east. For motorists in a hurry to reach their destination, *Great Exits* provides basic service information, and for travellers with time on their hands, it suggests a wide range of Ontario experiences beyond the next exit sign. Drive the 1000 Islands Parkway in the early winter when ice skins the surface of the bays and inlets. Start your Christmas shopping early at a factory outlet, or gain a perspective on the past from the century-old gravestones of early Canadians. *Great Exits* is "freeway friendly." It's portable. It's easy to use. And it informs.

The premise of *Great Exits* is simple. Any exit is great if it has what you need. I hope that readers of this book will share their own great exits with the rest of us. The criteria are simple. A great exit should be within an easy drive of a Highway 401 interchange—probably no more than 5 minutes and at the very maximum, 10 minutes. A great exit might be as obvious as a roadside service station, or it might be a place especially favoured by the locals. A great exit could be commercial or historic. A great exit can be as simple as a glowing patch of marsh marigolds. If you would like to share your great exits, write or fax me care of the publisher, and I will check out your suggestions for possible use in the next edition of *Great Exits*.

Boston Mills Press
132 Main Street,
Erin, Ontario N0B 1T0
Fax 519-833-2195

HIGHWAY 401

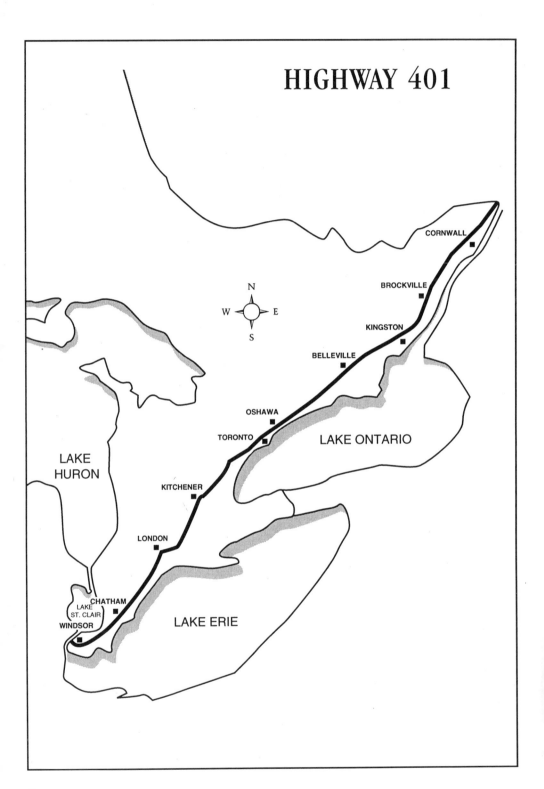

A History of Highway 401

Anyone born after 1960 can be forgiven for thinking that Highway 401 has always been there. But it isn't so! The route the 401 follows from Windsor to the eastern edge of Ontario is the product of years of meticulous research and co-ordinated planning. It is not an earlier King's Road revamped nor a Governor's Trail resurfaced, but a whole new roadway designed to accommodate the long-distance movement of goods and people across the province—a transprovincial expressway. The surrounding residential subdivisions, industries and shopping malls have since grown up around it.

It began in the 1930s when government planners looked at our limited provincial roadways, our burgeoning population and the growing popularity and affordability of automobiles. Canada's first four-lane controlled-access highway, the Queen Elizabeth Way from Toronto to Niagara Falls was completed in 1939. It was the beginning of a move away from local roadways to superhighways. When government funding for highway projects dried up with the outbreak of the Second World War, planners used the time to evaluate the design and construction of the QEW. The advances in heavy equipment developed during the war easily made up for lost time. With returning war veterans and a growing population clamouring for more automobiles and better roads, the heat was on and superhighway planning resumed.

As a preliminary step toward a transprovincial superhighway, 375,000 motorists were interviewed in an origin-destination survey to determine the preferred line of travel between points in Ontario. The route of Highway 401 is based on the replies to that early survey.

Planners followed one basic principle. Construction would not begin at one end of the province and work toward the other end. Instead, the highway would be built in sections as needed. As isolated sections were completed, they would be hooked up temporarily with existing highways until all the pieces of the puzzle were in place. A 300-foot (90 m) road allowance would be purchased, but in some instances only two lanes of the planned four would be built or opened until traffic conditions dictated the need for the additional lanes. When complete, the four lanes of Highway 401 would stretch across the province, a true freeway with no tolls and no obstructions. It was a plan of staggering dimensions.

The first 27-kilometre section, between eastern Toronto and Ritson Road in Oshawa, was completed in December 1947. More than 20 years later, in October of 1968, the last section, east of Gananoque to Highway 2 west of Brockville, was officially opened.

Each section of the highway required about 4 years of planning before construction could begin. Once the general route was established, engineers and surveyors scrutinized each proposed mile, seeking the most suitable path. They looked for eskers—mounds of gravel and sand deposited by retreating glaciers—because this kind of terrain provided a solid, elevated base. The planners also attempted to minimize farm disruption by building between concession lines at the back of adjoining farms. Municipalities along the route were asked for input. In the process, the planners encountered problems ranging from disgruntled, by-passed towns to demanding terrain.

A route through the Dorchester Swamp east of London, chosen to save prime farmland, required unique solutions. The organic material of the swamp was skimmed off and replaced with appropriate fill. The road base was built up 6 feet (2 m) above grade and then compressed to provide a stable base. In the last section east of Gananoque, planners built through, over and around the great granite outcrops. Although costly, this is one of the most scenic parts of Highway 401.

The original decision to prohibit service facilities along the freeway meant that motorists had to exit into nearby cities and towns for every fill-up and every sandwich. By 1961, the government could no longer ignore the public outcry—regulated, controlled-access service centres, open 24 hours a day, providing automobile and restaurant services and picnic areas, are now an integral part of Highway 401.

The Toronto By-pass, as the section across the top of the city was originally called, proved to be anything but a by-pass. In 1956 when the section was completed, planners expected to funnel 48,000 cars a day around the city. The magnetic attraction of the freeway for developers and the increasing numbers of commuters working far from home meant that the by-pass soon outgrew these expectations. Today, the Toronto By-pass has grown from four lanes stretching through farmers' fields to sixteen lanes hemmed in on all sides by development. A third of a million cars travel some part of the 42-kilometre stretch across the top of Toronto on an average weekday, making it the second busiest freeway in North America, second only to California's Santa Monica Freeway.

Lacking further road allowance to construct additional lanes to handle the continually increasing traffic, planners now concentrate on managing the traffic effectively. In a 16-kilometre stretch from Yonge

Street to Martin Grove Road, a network of roadway sensors relays information via electronic signals to banks of computers. Using the information from these computers and video images from remote cameras, operators can immediately direct service, police and medical teams to trouble spots. Messages on overhead signs change to reflect the current traffic conditions and warn motorists of trouble areas ahead.

Just as socio-economic patterns have changed as a result of our 20th-century mobility, the means for that mobility keeps changing. On Highway 401, lanes are widened, interchanges added and median barriers erected. The traffic never stops, nor do the changes. In 1965, in recognition of 19th-century Canadian nation builders Sir George-Étienne Cartier and Sir John A. Macdonald, Highway 401 was renamed the Macdonald-Cartier Freeway. How well the Macdonald-Cartier Freeway/Highway 401 accommodates increasing traffic in the coming century remains to be seen.

How to Use This Book

Where to Start

Great Exits describes the interchanges from west to east. The number of each interchange is the distance in kilometres from the Windsor starting point. Thus, Highway 59, Woodstock, which is 232 kilometres from the western beginning of Highway 401, is interchange number 232 (IC #232). Unlike the original numbering system in which the exits were numbered from 1 to 128, this current system allows travellers to easily determine their current position or destination distance. For example, to calculate the distance from the Port Hope Highway 28 interchange to Avenue Road in Toronto, subtract IC #367 (Avenue Road) from IC #464 (Port Hope). The distance between the two exits is 97 kilometres. Between interchanges, markers every couple of kilometres along the roadway give actual kilometre readings.

Travellers driving from east to west should begin at the back of the book. Since all "On the Road Again" information leads east from each interchange, westbound travellers should glance ahead one interchange to ensure they do not miss pertinent information.

A quick guide to roadside highway service centres is included for your reference on page 158, but I encourage you to use *Great Exits* to explore Ontario beyond these roadside centres.

Great Exits details information on all the interchanges from Windsor to the Quebec border with the exception of most interchanges across Metropolitan Toronto. On the one hand, basic services are available at virtually every Toronto interchange and the city's street-grid system makes returning to Highway 401 simple. On the other hand, travellers who are completely unfamiliar with the city may feel more comfortable exiting at one of the two Toronto interchanges described, or at interchanges on the western or eastern fringes of the city. The Toronto interchanges are listed in sequence on page 158.

Services

Great Exits lists the services available directly from Highway 401 interchanges. The distance is stated for services beyond a couple of kilometres. In built-up town and city areas, 5 minutes spent in traffic does not take you far off course. However, in rural Ontario you can drive a considerable distance in 5 minutes. Therefore time is not the only criterion for services listed, and how far is too far to be "directly off the 401" is my subjective decision.

In cities serviced by a number of 401 interchanges, usually one of the arterial streets has developed as a service corridor. The symbol ★ indicates the interchange with the greatest number of services.

For travellers with specific loyalties, the following companies are indicated by their logos.

Fast Food	Gasoline	Motel/Hotel Accommodation
HARVEY'S *Tim Hortons.* swiss chalet chicken +ribs McDonald's Burger King pizza pizza. KFC	PETRO-CANADA ® Shell Esso Sunoco	Comfort Inn Quality Inn DAYS INN *The Best Value Under The Sun.®* Quality Suites Quality Hotel Holiday Inn. Travelodge RAMADA

The following symbols represent all others:

Restaurants	Gasoline	Accommodation
🍴	⛽	🛏

A service symbol may represent one or many establishments. The appropriate service symbol is followed by the national-brand logo, if applicable. For example, the Shell gas station south at IC #509 is represented by ⛽ and (Shell)

The unidentified-brand gas station south at IC #522 is indicated with just ⛽

Other symbols used are

Fresh Produce (in Season)	Telephone in Car Pool Parking Lot	No Services Directly off the 401
🌽	☎	🚫

Points of Interest

Great Exits assumes that even a short break from the other gas-guzzlers on Highway 401 recharges the traveller's batteries. Possible diversions beyond the next exit sign are described briefly and their distance from the interchange is given, allowing you to make informed choices. Is a birding hotspot worth a 5-minute drive? Would the family enjoy a visit to an emu farm? Can a giant ice-cream cone relieve freeway fatigue?

The parameters for points of interest differ only slightly from those for available services. Most listed historic sites, antique shops, factory outlets and conservation areas are within 5 minutes of Highway 401; others, although up to 10 minutes from the highway, are included if I think they are particularly interesting. If a really note-worthy attraction is beyond even those limits, it is listed as "Further Afield."

The information provided in *Great Exits* is not all-inclusive, and although I have attempted to accommodate a wide variety of interests, my biases are probably apparent. Just as construction on Highway 401 never ceases, neither do the services at interchanges remain constant. Businesses come and go. Museums change their operating hours. Weather conditions affect the produce offered for sale at roadside stands. Restaurant hours are included only if they are unusually long or varied. The information on services and attractions is, to the best of my knowledge, correct at the time of writing.

Admission Charges

Great Exits does not list the cost of special attractions. It only states whether or not there are admission charges. Where possible, telephone numbers have been given to allow you to check specific charges.

Special Events and Seasonal Happenings

Great Exits encourages motorists to enjoy the changing seasons. Trilliums bloom for only a few short weeks in May. The chinook salmon swim up the Credit River only in late fall. Century-old fall fairs are over in a weekend.

Maps

Great Exits is not an atlas. Maps are not drawn to scale and are meant only as a guide to the relative positions of highways, streets and points of interest.

Information for the Road

Rules of the Road

1. The speed limit on Highway 401 is 100 kilometres per hour (60 mph). Heavy fines are levied on motorists exceeding the limit. Photo-radar units patrol sections of Highway 401 and a quick flash from an unmarked van may result in a speeding ticket in the mail a couple of weeks later.
2. The use of seat belts is mandatory in Ontario.
3. No stopping or parking on the side of the roadway is allowed except in an emergency.

Speed Conversion Chart

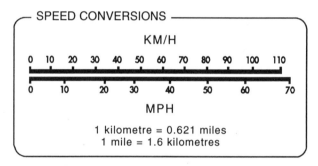

Car Pool Parking Lot Public Telephone Locations

The following car pool parking lots are equipped with public telephones. The parking lots are always directly off Highway 401 and easily accessed.

IC #286   Regional Road 33/Townline Road/Cambridge

IC #299   Highway 6 South/Hamilton/Brock Road/Guelph

IC #328   Trafalgar Road/Halton Hills/Georgetown/Oakville

IC #342   Highway 10/Brampton/Mississauga

IC #410   Highway 12/Brock Street/Whitby

IC #464   Highway 28/Bewdley/Port Hope/Peterborough

IC #474   Highway 45/Division Street/Cobourg/Baltimore

IC #497   Percy Street/Big Apple Drive/Colborne/Castleton

IC #509   Highway 30/Brighton/Campbellford

IC #522   Wooler Road/Northumberland Road 40

IC #611   Highway 38/Harrowsmith/Sharbot Lake

Public telephones are also located in vehicle-inspection stations.

CBC Radio Frequencies

Stay tuned to CBC across the width of the province.

Chatham . . . . 88.1 FM

Cornwall . . . . 99.5 FM

Kingston . . . . 107.5 FM

Kingston . . . . 92.9 FM (Stereo)

London . . . . 93.5 FM

London . . . . 100.5 FM (Stereo)

Ottawa. . . . . 91.5 FM (pick up east of Kingston)

Ottawa. . . . . 103.3 FM (Stereo)

Peterborough. . . . . . . 93.5 FM (pick up east of Toronto)

Peterborough. . . . . . . 103.9 FM (Stereo)

Toronto . . . . 740 AM

Toronto . . . . 94.1 FM (Stereo)

Windsor. . . . . 1550 AM

Windsor. . . . . 89.9 FM (Stereo)

Independent, private radio stations are listed in the *Great Exit* profiles.

Motel/Hotel Toll-Free 1-800 Numbers

Best Western Hotel. 1-800-528-1234

Choice Hotels 1-800-424-6423

   (Comfort Inn, Quality Inn, Quality Suites, Quality Hotel, Econo, Rodeway, Friendship, Clarion)

Days Inn 1-800-325-2525

Delta Inn 1-800-268-1133

Holiday Inn 1-800-465-4329

Howard Johnson Hotel 1-800-446-4656

Ramada Inn/Hotel. 1-800-544-9881

Travelodge 1-800-578-7878

Road Conditions Information

Throughout the province, call 1-800-268-1376 for up-to-date information on road conditions. In the Toronto area, call 416-235-1110. Cellular telephone users, call * 7623.

#013
Highway 401
Diversion to Tunnel/
Windsor

If you are beginning your trans-Ontario journey, IC #013 appears out of nowhere. Suddenly you are committed to travelling along Ontario's "main street," through the flat cornfields of Essex County, even perhaps as far as the industrial centres of central Ontario, or beyond. If IC #013 is your final exit, you'll notice that without any ceremony, the 401 just fades away.

Lucky IC #013 in Windsor, site of Canada's first and (at the time of writing) only casino, might be the beginning or the conclusion of an exciting odyssey.

Entering the 401: Travellers arriving in Windsor via the Ambassador Bridge can continue on Huron Church Road and then Talbot Road to the 401, whereas those emerging from the Windsor–Detroit Tunnel into downtown Windsor should take Ouellette Avenue south to the 401.

Exiting the 401: Westbound travellers have the same choices in reverse order. Where the 401 stops at Kilometre Thirteen, the highway divides. The Highway 3 fork leads to Huron Church Road and the bridge to the United States. The Highway 3B fork leads to Howard Avenue,

Dougall and Ouellette Avenues, downtown, the casino, and the tunnel to the United States. Each route offers a choice of restaurants, motels and gas stations.

Roll Back the Clock: The shores of the upper St. Lawrence and Lake Ontario are often assumed to be the earliest areas of settler expansion beyond Quebec, but the area around the Detroit River was settled earlier than many of the Loyalist areas of Ontario. By the early 1700s French pioneers were farming on the Canadian side of the river and their influence is still felt in the many bilingual Lake St. Clair communities.

Although the area's benign climate is favourable for agriculture, 20th-century Windsor is a major industrial city. With the large manufacturing facilities of Chrysler, Ford and General Motors, Windsor is recognized as the automotive capital of Canada.

The location of Highway 401 in relation to Windsor is a pattern that is repeated across the province. To by-pass city congestion, the 401 was constructed far beyond the city core. As a result, any route from the 401 to downtown Windsor will take more than 10 minutes.

Hospital: Windsor Western Hospital, Prince Road, off Huron Church Road, general 519-257-5100, emergency 519-257-5105. Hotel Dieu Grace Hospital, 1030 Ouellette Avenue, general 519-973-4444, emergency 519-973-4400.

Radio Stations: CKLW 800 AM, CKWW 580 AM, CIMX 89X 88.7 FM, CKLW 93.9 FM

Tourist Information: Ontario Travel Information Centres are open daily at the Windsor–Detroit Tunnel at 110 Park Street East, 519-973-1338, and at the Ambassador Bridge at 1235 Huron Church Road East, 519-973-1310. Victoria Day to Labour Day, 8 A.M. to 8 P.M.; rest of the year, 8:30 A.M. to 4:30 P.M.

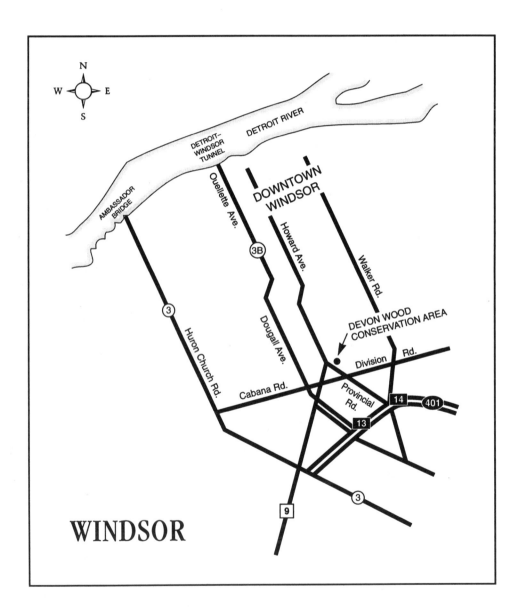

INTERCHANGE

#014
Essex Road 46/
Windsor

The 10-kilometre drive north on Walker Road to the eastern area of downtown Windsor can easily take 15 minutes. Close to Riverside Drive are the Ottawa Street shops and restaurants; Willistead Manor, the impressive former Walker home, built early in this century by Hiram Walker's son Edward; and the Hiram Walker Distillery and tour facilities.

➤ SOUTH
Services:

Husky Service Centre, open 24 hours

➤ NORTH
Services: In first 2.5 kilometres to Division Street

 PETRO-CANADA®

Take a Hike: From Walker Road turn left onto Division Road and continue on Division as it forks north from Cabana Road.

Devonwood, a 94-acre (38 ha) wooded conservation area, contains the largest variety of oak species in Canada: white, chinquapin, bur, swamp white, pin, shumard, red and black oak. Hiking trails. No charge.

Special Events: Canada's most southern city has the distinction of looking north to the United States, and once a year Windsor shares a festival with its northern neighbour, Detroit. The annual 10-day International Freedom Festival (519-252-7264), beginning late June, celebrates each country's national holiday, Canada Day on July 1st and Independence Day on July 4th.

On the Road Again: Retrace your route on Walker Road or follow Howard or Dougall Avenue to return to the 401 at IC #013. Riverside Drive, or Highway 2 east, meets Essex Road 19 for a return to the 401 at IC #021.

INTERCHANGE

#021
Essex Road 19/
Tecumseh

Leaving Windsor, Highway 401 begins a rural route across the flat Essex plain far from the shoreline towns of Lake Erie. Tecumseh (population 10,500), 10 kilometres north, is the first of many lakeside towns east of Windsor. Maidstone (population 860) is 4 kilometres south of the 401 in the heart of Essex County farmland.

➤ SOUTH

Services:

The Cozy Corner Restaurant, a family-style restaurant at the intersection of County Roads 19 and 34, is a popular local spot. Open Sunday through Wednesday 6:30 A.M. to 8 P.M.; Thursday through Saturday 6:30 A.M. to 1 P.M., 519-723-4433.
OPP: Just south on County Road 19, 519-776-5276.

Off the Beaten Track: A few years ago, volunteers from the Essex County Field Naturalists began collecting seeds of tree species native to Carolinian forests in a long-range plan to reforest local areas. On the southwest corner of this interchange, you can see the 3-year-old, spindly seedlings grown from the first collected seeds and transplanted here in November 1994. They represent local conservation efforts to ensure the continued presence of the unique species of Carolinian Canada.

➤ NORTH

Services:

  at 4.5 kilometres

All services in Tecumseh.

Special Events: With the possible closing of the Green Giant processing plant in Tecumseh, the hugely successful Tecumseh Green Giant Corn Festival (519-735-2184) is in jeopardy. Plans are in place for the 4-day event in Lacasse Park on the last weekend in August 1995, but no one knows whether it will continue in

Love Apples

In September, trails of road-kill tomatoes lead from Southwestern Ontario fields where tons of the ripe, red love apples are being machine-picked, sorted and loaded onto open transports for their last ride. Next stop, ketchup and tomato juice. Tomatoes are the favourite vegetable of home gardeners. Since only the pale pink imported variety are available for many months of the year, we crave the sun-soaked, locally grown ones. Tomatoes were introduced to Europe by the conquistadors who had learned of the fruit from the Indians of Central and South America, and were soon adopted by the French and the Italians. But of all the native American vegetables, tomatoes were the last to gain acceptance in North America. Corn, beans and even squash got the nod before tomatoes. According to one theory, early settlers, confusing the instructions, ate the poisonous foliage and thus the whole plant got a bad reputation.

future years. In the past, tens of thousands of visitors have found the entertainment and hot, buttered corn-on-the-cob "ear-resistable."

On the Road Again: If you want more of rural Ontario, take County Road 46 east. It runs south of, and parallel to, the 401. Return to the 401 at IC #028 or IC #034.

#028
Puce Road/Essex
Road 25/Puce/Essex

Puce Road leads north to another Lake St. Clair community, Puce. The town of Essex (population 6,600) is beyond our reach to the south.

➢ SOUTH

Take a Hike: Drive south about 3 kilometres to County Road 46. Cross County Road 46 and continue on the unpaved road for a few hundred feet. Maidstone Conservation Area is on the right. The woodlot's oak and hickory trees are representative of the distinct plant life of Carolinian Canada. About halfway around the walking trail, a shagbark hickory tree demonstrates real perseverance. The tree grows upright for a metre or so, makes a 90-degree

bend, and grows parallel to the ground for a couple of metres before it makes another 90-degree turn and grows upright again. Amazingly, the horizontal section is hollow, and few visitors can resist the temptation to push their faces up to the hole. Beware the forest creatures who might consider your action trespassing! Picnic facilities. Washroom. No charge.

➢ NORTH

Follow the North Star: The Underground Railroad was a secret system by which antislavery sympathizers helped thousands of slaves escape to the northern United States and Canada during the early 19th century and until the Civil War. Throughout Southwestern Ontario, communities of freed and fugitive slaves settled and flourished. Their struggles and successes are documented at historic sites designated with the symbol of the North Star. At the John Freeman Walls Historic Site, 2 kilometres north on Puce Road, the log cabin built in 1846 by John Freeman Walls is the nucleus of an Underground Railroad museum operated by his descendants. Open July to Labour Day, daily 10 A.M. to 5 P.M. Admission charge.

On the Road Again: As you backtrack to the 401 from Maidstone Conservation Area, notice how the jogs in County Road 25 resemble the turns taken by the shagbark hickory trunk.

#034
Belle River Road/
Essex Road 27/
Woodslee/Belle River

North Woodslee and South Woodslee are crossroad communities to the south. Jack Miner's Bird Sanctuary is 21 kilometres south, near Kingsville. Belle River, a community founded by French soldiers who did not return home after the fall of New France in 1770, is located 6.5 kilometres north on the shore of Lake St. Clair.

➤ SOUTH

➤ NORTH

Services: In Belle River

Antiques: West on Highway 2 (less than 2 kilometres), Fern & Linda's Antiques, at 1537 Highway 2, is open 10 A.M. to 6 P.M. every day except Wednesday, 519-727-6710.

Picnic in the Park: At the foot of Belle River Road, just north of Highway 2, a sandy beach and park area on Lake St. Clair are accessible to the public. Swimming, picnic facilities, washrooms, parking. West on Highway 2, the Optimists' Park has playground equipment and picnic facilities, but no access to the lake.

On the Road Again: From County Road 46 east, south of the 401, a return to the 401 is easy at any of the next three interchanges. To the north, County Road 2 and Highway 2 follow a circuitous eastern route.

#040
St. Joachim Road/
Essex Road 31/
St. Joachim

The land in Essex County is flatter than flat and nowhere is this more apparent than on the drive to St. Joachim. From the moment you head north from the 401, the church, 4.5 kilometres away, is clearly visible.

➤ SOUTH

➤ NORTH

Services: In St. Joachim

#048
Highway 77
Comber/Stoney Point/
Leamington

Highway 401 continues east, parallel to the Lake St. Clair shoreline, but still a bit far from the lakeside communities for a quick dip. In Stoney Point (Pointe aux Roches), bilingual signs indicate a strong Francophone presence. Leamington is 24 kilometres south on Highway 77 on the shore of Lake Erie.

➤ SOUTH
Services:

 Sunoco

For the Birds: Comber may be a tiny town but it has a big reputation among birders. During spring migration (usually the month of May), in the area behind the Big O Drain Tile Company, migrating birds stop for a breather after crossing Lake Erie. Northern parula, prothonotary, cerulean and hooded warblers may visit here. Turn left at County Road 46, then right on Windsor Avenue and follow the gravel road back behind the tile company. A sign points the way.

Walking trails provide access to a poplar and maple bush, swamps, marshland and a pond. No charge. The Crossroads Restaurant (519-687-3411) records sightings in a logbook.

➤ NORTH
Services: In Stoney Point, 7 kilometres north

On the Road Again: Highway 2 east leads directly into Tilbury and the 401.

#056
Highway 2/
West of Tilbury

Highways 2 and 401 intersect and cross on either side of Tilbury. Highway 2 west parallels the 401 on the north whereas Highway 2 east dips south of the 401 and leads directly into the town of Tilbury (population 4,300). Tilbury's origins date to the building of the Canadian Southern Railway in 1872, but many forces have shaped its growth. The town's proximity to the 401 may be the latest influence, but a variety of factors have affected its

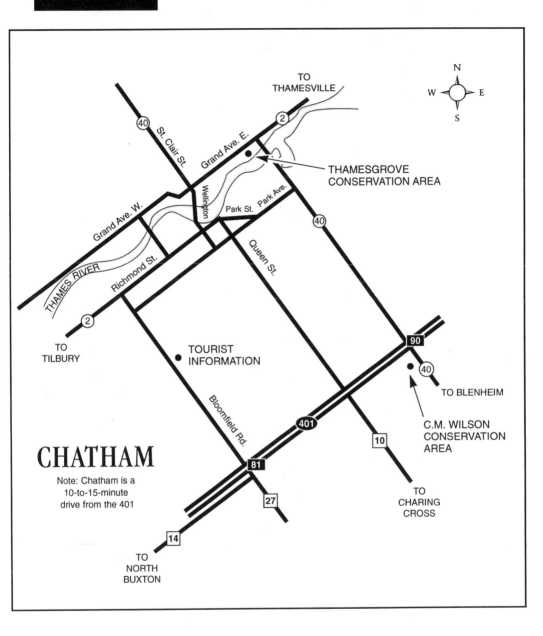

CHATHAM

Note: Chatham is a
10-to-15-minute
drive from the 401

development: its location in one of the country's richest agricultural areas and the resulting food processing facilities; the demands of prospectors and speculators in the early oil boom to the north; and the establishment of auto-related industries to support the auto industry in Windsor.

➤ EAST
Services:

➢ WEST

Services: On Highway 2 west

On the Road Again: Follow Highway 2 through Tilbury and return to the 401 at the eastern entrance to town, IC #063.

INTERCHANGE

#063
Highway 2/
East of Tilbury

Highway 2 to the southwest leads to Tilbury, 6 kilometres away (see IC #056).

Highway 2 to the northeast leads to Chatham (22 kilometres), with few services along the way.

On the Road Again: For those travelling east, an alternate route to Chatham is to follow Highway 2 northeast to the intersection with County Road 7. Turn right (or south) and proceed on County Road 7 to its

intersection with County Road 14. Turn left (east) and follow County Road 14 to North Buxton and the Raleigh Township Centennial Museum, a museum celebrating the memory of the Elgin Settlement. See IC #081.

INTERCHANGE

#081
Bloomfield Road/Kent
Road 27/Chatham

Bloomfield Road leads north to Chatham (population 43,000) and directly south to Lake Erie. Eastbound travellers should take this exit for Chatham.

In his efforts to replicate the mother country and demonstrating a singular lack of imagination, Lieutenant-Governor John Graves Simcoe, the British government's representative in late 18th-century Canada, named the colonial river the Thames and the settlement near its mouth, Chatham.

➢ SOUTH

Follow the North Star: Take County Road 27 to County Road 14 and turn right. Follow County Road 14 for 7.5 kilometres to North Buxton, a hamlet of fewer than 200 people. In the mid-1800s, with the support and encouragement of

25

Reverend William King, an abolitionist, North Buxton flourished as a 2,000-strong, self-supporting, all-Black community. The Raleigh Township Centennial Museum in the former school preserves the history of this settlement of freed slaves known as the Elgin Settlement. Open May 1 to September 30, Wednesday through Sunday 1 P.M. to 4:30 P.M. Admission charge, 519-352-4799. A few kilometres farther south in South Buxton (the intersection of County Roads 8 and 6), St. Andrew's Presbyterian Church and the house across the street, that of former slave George Hatter, date to the same period.

➤ NORTH

Services: 5 kilometres to Bloomfield Road and Richmond Street (Highway 2)

Downtown Chatham is another 4 kilometres east along Richmond Street and although it is 10 minutes from the 401, as the hub of Kent County, it can provide most services.

Hospital: Chatham General Hospital, 106 Emma Street, 519-352-6400; St. Joseph's Hospital, 519 King Street West, 519-352-2500.

Newspaper: *The Chatham Daily News*

Radio Stations: CFCO 630 AM, CKSY FM 95

Tourist Information: A seasonal visitor information centre operates on Bloomfield Road at Hitchcock Road from May till September, 11 A.M. to 7 P.M. Year-round information is available at the Civic Centre, 315 King Street West, Monday through Friday 9 A.M. to 5 P.M. 1-800-561-6125.

Roll Back the Clock: Chatham is a pretty town along the banks of the Thames River with wonderful old brick houses on maple-shaded streets, museums, riverside parks and an intriguing past. Begun as a naval dockyard in 1793 and later settled by Loyalists, Chatham became a terminus of the Underground Railroad and the largest centre for the Black population in Ontario in the mid-1800s. It was here in 1848 at the First Baptist Church that John Brown planned his ill-fated insurgence against the American government, leading to his capture at Harper's Ferry and his subsequent execution for treason.

Play Awhile: The Wheels Inn at 615 Richmond Street (east of Bloomfield Road) provides Best Western hotel accommodation and an indoor adventure for the whole family. Water slides, the Gorilla Golf and Games Reserve, and the recently opened Wild Zone are all part of the entertainment complex. Some activities are restricted to hotel guests. 1-800-265-5257. Open all year.

For Art's Sake: Visit the Chatham Cultural Centre, the Thames Art Gallery and the Chatham Kent Museum at 75 William Street (in downtown Chatham across from Tecumseh Park). Open Tuesday through Sunday 1 P.M. to 5 P.M. No charge, 519-354-8338.

On the Road Again: From downtown Chatham, return to the 401 on Highway 40, IC #090.

INTERCHANGE

#090
Highway 40
Chatham/Blenheim

Westbound travellers enroute to Chatham should exit at this interchange and return to the 401 via Bloomfield Road, IC #081. Chatham is about 12 kilometres north on Highway 40. Blenheim, a farming community of 4,500, is 10 kilometres to the south. For other information on Chatham, see IC #081.

➤ SOUTH

Take a Hike: To reach the C.W. Wilson Conservation Area (3.6 kilometres from the 401), turn right at Horton Road, just south of the 401, and continue west to the railway tracks. Turn right immediately after the tracks. The park offers picnic facilities, fishing, nature trails, swimming, a park store and washrooms. During the construction of the 401, large amounts of gravel and soil were needed to build up ramps and adjoining roads, and where possible the required soil was excavated nearby. Often the resulting "borrow pits" filled with water, creating ponds. Here, at C.W. Wilson Conservation Area, one such pond is used as a recreational facility. Admission charge between Victoria Day and Labour Day.

➤ NORTH

OPP: On Park Avenue East off Highway 40, 519-352-1122.

Antiques: Dorothy's Country Antiques, on the right side of Highway 40 just north of the 401, is open most days from Wednesday through Sunday, 519-352-0337.

Step Back in Time: Catch a glimpse of the steam era by visiting the Chatham Railroad Museum. The museum is in a retired 1955 CN baggage car on McLean Street at Queen and William Streets. Open May to September, Monday through Friday 9 A.M. to 5 P.M.; Saturday and Sunday noon to 5 P.M. No charge, 519-352-3097.

Special Events: On the first weekend in October, the Thamesgrove Conservation Area is transformed into an Upper Canada village of 1813. The fateful Battle of the Thames, in which the great Shawnee war chief Tecumseh disappeared and was believed killed in action, is reenacted here. Continue on Highway 40 to Highway 2 (Grand Avenue). Turn left on Grand Avenue and left again on Kingsway Avenue. Admission charge, 519-351-2058.

On the Road Again: County Road 14, just to the north of 401, leads east to McKay's Corners. See IC # 101.

#101
Kent Road 15/
McKay's Corners/
Kent Bridge/Dresden

McKay's Corners (population 90) is 2 kilometres to the north. Rondeau Provincial Park is 18 kilometres south through typical Southwestern Ontario farmland.

➤ SOUTH

➤ NORTH
Services: In McKay's Corners

Bargain Hunt: Just west of the four-corners community of McKay's Corners, the Village Barn Flea Market advertises everything from A to Z, new and used. Take your chances, Monday through Friday 9 A.M. to 5 P.M.; Saturday 10 A.M. to 4 P.M.; Sunday 11 A.M. to 4 P.M. McKay's Corners Surplus Centre offers drapes, fabrics, carpets, trims and notions, Monday through Friday 10 A.M. to 9 P.M.; Saturday 10 A.M. to 6 P.M.

Further Afield: Rondeau Provincial Park, a peninsula of land jutting into Lake Erie, is Ontario's second oldest park. It's big—8,040 acres (3,254 ha) of beaches, marshes, sloughs and forests—and the wildlife is abundant. The largest Canadian breeding ground of prothonotary warblers is located in the park. Carolinian flora and fauna are park trademarks. Hiking trails, picnic and swimming facilities and interpretive programs. Admission charge, 519-674-5405.

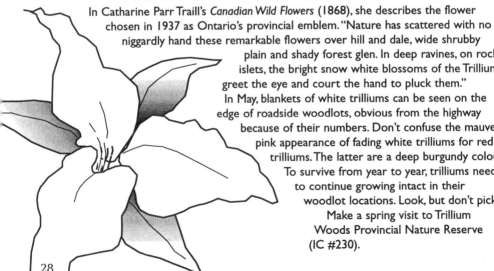

White Trillium

In Catharine Parr Traill's *Canadian Wild Flowers* (1868), she describes the flower chosen in 1937 as Ontario's provincial emblem. "Nature has scattered with no niggardly hand these remarkable flowers over hill and dale, wide shrubby plain and shady forest glen. In deep ravines, on rocky islets, the bright snow white blossoms of the Trilliums greet the eye and court the hand to pluck them."

In May, blankets of white trilliums can be seen on the edge of roadside woodlots, obvious from the highway because of their numbers. Don't confuse the mauve-pink appearance of fading white trilliums for red trilliums. The latter are a deep burgundy colour. To survive from year to year, trilliums need to continue growing intact in their woodlot locations. Look, but don't pick! Make a spring visit to Trillium Woods Provincial Nature Reserve (IC #230).

#109
Highway 21/
Ridgetown/Thamesville

The ridge that divides the north and south watersheds of the area gives Ridgetown (population 3,200) its name. Ridgetown's past is well-preserved in the Ridge House Museum on Erie Street South; the area's future is in the hands of student farmers studying modern agricultural techniques at the Ridgetown College of Agricultural Technology. Ridgetown is 6.5 kilometres south of the 401.

Thamesville, 10 kilometres to the north, takes its name from the Battle of the Thames fought nearby during the War of 1812.

➢ SOUTH

Services:

Most services in Ridgetown, including Lilly's Tea Room & Gifts at 11 Main Street, 519-674-3814.
OPP: On Erie Street in Ridgetown, 519-674-5496.
Newspaper: *Ridgetown Dominion*, weekly on Wednesdays.

Tourist Information: A bright yellow railway car sidelined directly south of the 401 puts travellers on the right track. Seasonal. Open mid-May to Labour Day, daily 9 A.M. to 8 P.M.

For the Birds: Take Erie Street north from the main intersection about 1.5 kilometres to Kent County Fertilizer Ltd. Turn left at Mitton Line and continue to the viewing platform on the left. A sewage pond might seem an unsavory birding site, but shorebirds are attracted to the abundance of invertebrate food in these lagoons.

Picnic in the Park: Watson's Park, with picnic facilities and washrooms, is just off Main Street on York Street, west of Erie Street.

Fair Days: Ridgetown's fair takes place the first weekend in August.

Further Afield: At Romoe Restorick's Buffalo Head Ranch on Golf Course Road, just west of Erie Street, the buffalo do roam. Mind the signs and be satisfied with the view from the road. Visit the trading post to stock up on frozen meat—buffalo, venison and wild boar. Tours of the ranch must be arranged in advance, 519-674-0320.

➢ NORTH

On the Road Again: Take County Road 19 east, off Highway 21, between the 401 and Ridgetown, and return to the 401 at IC #117, just north of Highgate.

#117
Highgate Road/
Kent Road 20/Highgate

Rural Ontario stretches farther than the eye can see in all directions from this interchange. In the village of Highgate (population 500), 2 kilometres south, the redbrick Highgate United Church was built in 1918 to replace the former Methodist church founded in 1898. It has an unusual rounded entry and lovely stained-glass windows.

➤ **SOUTH**

Services:

➤ **NORTH**

On the Road Again: About 10 kilometres east on Highway 401 from the Highgate interchange, look carefully at the cornfields on both sides of the road. You'll see a string of oil rigs, monotonously pumping up and down, taking oil from fields that have been producing for over a hundred years. In Oil Springs, about 60 kilometres northwest, the Oil Museum of Canada documents the industry's history. The locals had long been aware of natural asphalt in the area's tarry gum beds when, in 1855–56, Charles Tripp loaded seven ships with asphalt destined to pave the streets of Paris. The presence of asphalt often indicates oil, and in 1858 in Oil Springs, James Miller Williams sank the first commercial oil well in North America. In late summer and fall, the rigs disappear behind the tall stalks of corn.

#129
Furnival Road/
Elgin Road 3/
Rodney/Wardsville

The yellow-brick village of Rodney (population 1,000) is 2 kilometres south of the 401 in the rich farmland of Elgin County. The town's name was chosen in 1875 to honour Admiral Lord Rodney of the Royal Navy.

➤ Westbound travellers should read IC #117 "On the Road Again" before proceeding past this interchange.

➤ **SOUTH**

Services:

Fair Days: In 1994, the 140th annual Rodney–Aldborough Fair was held as usual on the third weekend in September. Look for it next year, same time, same place.

➤ NORTH

#137
Highway 76/
West Lorne

More rural Ontario! Highway 2 intersects Highway 76, 11 kilometres north. Two small communities, West Lorne (population 1,400) and Eagle (population 58), are south on Highway 76.

➤ SOUTH
Services: In West Lorne

Newspaper: *The West Lorne Sun,* weekly on Wednesday.

Off the Beaten Track: There are at least two good reasons for driving 6 kilometres out of your way to Eagle, the crossroads community beyond West Lorne. The Ol' Country Store, a general store with everything from plumbing supplies to videos, serves huge ice-cream cones. The double-scoops are only for the very ambitious. Open daily, Monday

through Saturday 8 A.M. to 10 P.M.; Sunday 9 A.M. to 10 A.M., 519-768-1600.

Gardeners can swoon over acres of greenery at Swain Greenhouses and then head next door to the Texas Longhorn Bar and Grill Restaurant and plan their gardening strategy. Open Monday through Saturday 9 A.M. to 5:30 P.M.; Sunday 10 A.M. to 6 P.M., 519-768-1116.

➤ NORTH

On the Road Again: Instead of returning to the 401, follow Highway 3 east to Wallacetown for a choice of two parks. At McKillop Side Road, turn south. The E.M. Warwick Conservation Area, 3 kilometres south on the north shore of Lake Erie, has a nature trail, an observation tower, picnic areas, washrooms, and lake access for swimming. Farther along on Highway 3, a pretty roadside park provides picnic and washroom facilities. Fresh produce in season is available at the roadside stands all along Highway 3.

#149
Currie Road/
Elgin Road 8/Dutton

Dutton, just off Highway 401, and Wallacetown, a bit farther south on County Road 8, are picturesque agricultural communities.

➤ SOUTH

Services: In Dutton

In Wallacetown

OPP: Just south on County Road 8, 519-762-2833.

Newspaper: *The Dutton Advance,* weekly on Wednesday.

Special Event: Dutton has an old-time town crier who spreads the news on Saturdays from Easter to Thanksgiving.

Tourist Information: At the Village Crier Gallery & Frame Shop, 194 Main Street, tourist information is available year-round. Open Monday to Wednesday and Saturday 9 A.M. to 6 P.M., Thursday and Friday 9 A.M. to 9 P.M., and Sunday 1 P.M. to 4 P.M.

Fair Days: The Wallacetown Fair takes place the last weekend in September.

➤ NORTH

On the Road Again: To soak up some down-on-the-farm atmosphere, take either Highway 3 east from Wallacetown or County Road 13 east from Dutton toward Iona and Iona Station.

INTERCHANGE

#157
Iona Road/Iona/ Melbourne

The stretch of 401 between Windsor and London cuts through quintessential rural Ontario. Iona Station and Iona, south from this interchange, are little more than crossroad communities.

➤ SOUTH

Services:

At the Holland House Restaurant and Gift Shop at the intersection of Highway 3 and County Road 14 (6 kilometres south of the 401), you can browse in the antique and gift shop while waiting for your choice of Canadian, Dutch or Indonesian food. Open daily 8 A.M. to 8 P.M., 519-764-2495.

Take a Hike: Watch for the sign for the Crane Conservation Area south on Iona Road, almost opposite the right turn to County Road 13 to Dutton. Small parking area and limited facilities. No charge.

Off the Beaten Track: From Iona, take County Road 14 south past Iona Commons General, an antique and

Carolinian Canada

Some call it the banana belt. Naturalists call it Carolinian Canada. It's a stretch of Ontario from the Rouge River Valley east of Toronto to Lake Erie and Windsor, an area that enjoys a relatively mild climate and supports, in a diverse variety of habitats, a wealth of unique species. Hooded warblers, southern flying squirrels, Acadian fly catchers, and North America's only marsupial, the opossum, live in this eastern deciduous forest that stretches as far south as the Carolinas. Kentucky coffee trees thrive in the area and the fringed polygala blooms here in the spring. Unfortunately, 90 percent of the habitat it takes to keep Carolinian species happy, healthy and safe has disappeared. What the early settlers didn't chop down, 20th-century development levelled. The biggest challenge confronting Carolinian species is this loss of habitat. In the protected environment of provincial and national parks, such as Rondeau and Point Pelee, you can still familiarize yourself with the wildlife native to Carolinian Canada. Take the opportunity—these species may not be around forever.

variety store located in an 1888 building, and continue for another 3 kilometres to the Southwold Earthworks. Even though only the earthworks of the ancient, double-walled village remain, the area still evokes a powerful presence of the past. Historians believe a village of Neutral Indians, perhaps as many as 800, lived here peaceably sometime between 1500 and the demise of their nation by 1650. Bring along a picnic to enjoy under the shade of the spreading beech trees. Picnic facilities and washrooms. No charge. **Further Afield:** A sign directly below the Earthworks' marker points to an eagle's nest to the west. It's a few kilometres away and might not be worth the time once the leaves are out in full. However, visitors here in the early spring, when the birds are likely to be on

the nest or nearby, have a reasonable chance of sightings. The eagles usually remain in the area till late August/early September.

Just beyond the Earthworks on County Road 14, turn right on Dunwich Township Concession 10 and proceed for 4 kilometres to the farm of Lyle and Mary Jones. A pair of bald eagles nested at this platform site until 1993 when they abandoned the site for another, 1.5 kilometres to the east. To locate the nest at the original site, look 100 feet (30 m) south into the woodlot beyond the markers, to the top of the trees. The new site is not marked but can be seen to the southwest from the culvert at Talbot Creek. It, too, is about 100 feet (30 m) into the woodlot. Binoculars are a big help. Unfortunately, eagle experts have no way of determining which nest site will be used in future years. Did you know that the "bald" of bald eagles refers not to the lack of feathers on their heads, but to their white head-feathers?

➤ NORTH

Off the Beaten Track: In the Cowal–McBride's Cemetery, 1 kilometre north, 19th-century headstones for McCallums and McNabbs are signs of the area's Scottish beginnings.

On the Road Again: If you plan to stop in St. Thomas, do not go back to Highway 401. Just continue east on Highway 3 from Iona.

opened in 1984 as the Old School House Tea Room, serving lunches and teas from a menu written on the blackboard. Open Tuesday through Sunday 10 A.M. to 4:30 P.M., 519-764-2272.

Next door, the Village Pantry Boutique, operated by the same family, offers antiques, books, crafts and craft supplies. Open Tuesday through Sunday 10 A.M. to 5 P.M., 519-764-2777. Both establishments are closed from Christmas Eve till the first Tuesday in February.

➤ NORTH

On the Road Again: From the south continue east on Highway 3 to St. Thomas.

INTERCHANGE

#164
Union Road/
Elgin Road 20/Shedden

More rural Ontario!

➤ SOUTH

Services: In Shedden, 5 kilometres south

Area children began learning their three Rs in Shedden's one-room schoolhouse in 1866. The last classes passed through 100 years later. Refurbished and restored, the school

INTERCHANGE

#177
Highway 4/
St. Thomas/London

Highway 4 north connects with Highway 402, the northwest express-way route to Sarnia, and then continues into London. See IC #186. This exit is the only opportunity for eastbound travellers to access Highway 402.

Eleven kilometres south is St. Thomas, with its yellow-brick, Victorian buildings. The Hill, with its statue of Jumbo, the famous circus elephant, and the tourist information centre, can be reached within 10 minutes. The rest of St. Thomas is a bit beyond our reach.

➤ SOUTH
Services:

All services in St. Thomas.

The Talbot Trail Restaurant & Gift Shop on the Hill at 86 Talbot Street is highly recommended for its great home-cooked food. One room of the 1855 building is devoted to a miniature circus display and a collection of circus memorabilia. Open Tuesday through Friday 7:30 A.M. to 7:30 P.M.; Saturday and Sunday 9 A.M. to 7:30 P.M., 519-633-8040.

Hospital: St. Thomas–Elgin General Hospital, 189 Elm Street, 519-631-2020.

Newspaper: *St. Thomas Times-Journal*, daily.

Radio Station: CFHK FM 103.1

Tourist Information: A travel information centre is operated seasonally in a caboose parked next to Jumbo at the top of Talbot Street. At the northwest edge of town, turn right off Highway 4 onto Talbot Street. Open mid-June to mid-October, Monday through Wednesday and

Saturday and Sunday 10 A.M. to 6 P.M. Open July and August daily 10 A.M. to 8 P.M. As well, the St. Thomas–Elgin Tourist Association at 555 Talbot Street is open year-round, Monday through Friday 8:30 A.M. to 5 P.M., 519-631-8188.

As Large as Life: The statue of Jumbo, P.T. Barnum's star attraction, was sculpted in 1985 a century after the circus elephant died here. Reputed to be the largest African elephant in captivity, Jumbo travelled with Barnum's circus for 20 years until that fateful night, September 15, 1885, in St. Thomas, when he was mortally wounded in a collision with a Grand Trunk locomotive.

Step Back in Time: Explore various aspects of Elgin County's past in the museums and historic buildings on Jumbo's Hill. The Elgin Military Museum at 30 Talbot Street, (open Tuesday through Sunday, afternoons) traces local military participation from the War of 1812 to the present. The Elgin County Pioneer Museum, 32 Talbot Street displays pioneer artefacts. Open Tuesday through Friday 10 A.M. to noon and 1 P.M. to 5 P.M.; Saturday and Sunday 2 P.M. to 5 P.M. Mary Rose Sanderson's Studio is located in the oldest brick building in St. Thomas at 76 Talbot Street. Open Tuesday through Saturday 10 A.M. to 5 P.M.; Sunday noon to 5 P.M., with extended summer hours. The Old St. Thomas Church, a block away on Walnut Street, was built in 1824 and has recently undergone a complete restoration.

➢ NORTH

Services:

Pick a Peck: Within 3 kilometres of the 401, three fruit and vegetable markets offer a variety of fresh products in season. Fondel's, just north, advertises pick-your-own fruit. Thomas Bros. Market, next on the right, carries a large selection of produce. A little farther along, Farmer Jack's offers pony rides for the kids while you choose your apples or pick your own.

INTERCHANGE

#183
Highway 402/
Sarnia

Highway 402 leads only in a north-westerly direction toward Sarnia. There is no access from the east-bound 401 to IC #183. Eastbound travellers who want to take Highway 402 should exit at IC #177. West-bound travellers wanting access to Lambeth or the western area of London can exit onto Highway 402 and then exit from it at the first interchange (IC #98).

INTERCHANGE

#186
Wellington Road
(to Highway 135)/
London

Wellington Road is the major artery into London (population 316,000). Downtown London is a 15-minute drive along Wellington Road from the 401 because the highway skirts the southern edge of the city. Also see IC #189 for London.

➢ SOUTH

Services:

➢ NORTH

Services: On Wellington Road and Exeter Street (also known as Highway 135), all services within a few minutes of the 401.

On Wellington Road

  Burger King

 Sunoco

Whiteoaks Mall (200-plus stores)

On Exeter Road

 Tim Hortons.

 Holiday Inn

OPP: Directly north of the 401, 519-681-0300.

Hospitals: Victoria Hospital (children's emergency), 800 Commissioners Road East, 519-685-8141. Victoria Hospital (adult emergency), South Street, 519-667-6529.

Newspaper: *London Free Press*, daily.

Radio Stations: CFPL AM 980, FM96 95.9, CKSL AM 1410, CJBX AM 1290, BX93 FM 92.7, Q-97.5 FM 97.5

Tourist Information: The city of London operates a year-round tourist information centre at 696 Wellington Road. Open Victoria Day through Labour Day, daily 8 A.M. to 8 P.M.; after Labour Day through Thanksgiving, daily 10 A.M. to 1 P.M. and 2 P.M. to 6 P.M. The rest of the year, Friday, Saturday and Sunday, the same hours as those from Labour Day to Thanksgiving. Washrooms. 1-800-265-2602.

Factory Outlets: Ask for the up-to-date listing of all factory outlets in the London area at the tourist information centre. Two outlets close to the 401 are *Florsheim Canada*, 824 Exeter Road, men's and ladies' shoes, open Monday through Friday 9 A.M. to 5:30 P.M.; Saturday 9 A.M. to 5 P.M., 519-681-0530; and the *Black and Decker Factory Store*, 981 Wellington Road, power tools and small appliances, open Monday through Friday 9:30 A.M. to 6 P.M.; Saturday 9 A.M. to 2 P.M.; 519-649-2407.

Bargain Hunt: The Wellington Flea Market at 824 Exeter Road is open Saturday and Sunday 9 A.M. to 5 P.M., 519-668-5700.

Play Awhile: It is pushing the 10-minute limit to reach either of these two attractions, but they are worth the extra time if children need some activity.

For Wally World, a world of wet and dry amusements at 1158 Wonderland Road South (519-473-1737), take Exeter Road West, turn north on Wonderland Road and continue to Southdale. The wet attractions are open from late May till early September, Monday through Friday 10 A.M. to 7 P.M.; Saturday and Sunday till 8 P.M. The season for dry attractions is extended. Admission charge.

Storybook Gardens, a theme park, play area and petting zoo, is located in Springbank Park. Take Wellington Road north to Commissioners Road and turn left, or access the park by continuing north on Wonderland Road beyond Wally World. Open May to September, daily 10 A.M. to 8 P.M.; September to mid-October, weekdays 10 A.M. to 5 P.M. and till 6 P.M. on weekends. Admission charge, 519-661-5770.

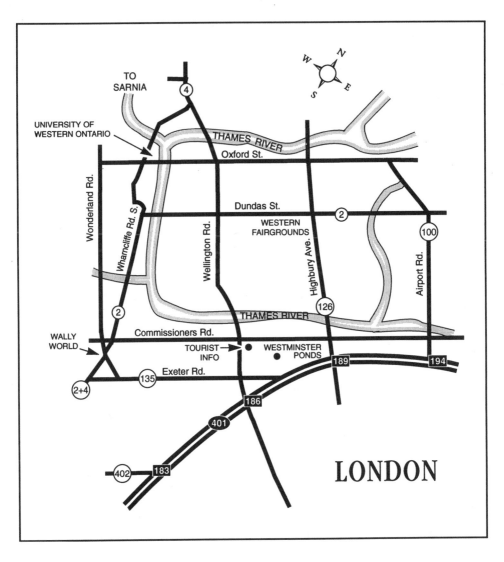

TO SARNIA

UNIVERSITY OF WESTERN ONTARIO

THAMES RIVER

Oxford St.

Wonderland Rd.

Wharncliffe Rd. S.

Wellington Rd.

Dundas St.

WESTERN FAIRGROUNDS

Highbury Ave.

Airport Rd.

THAMES RIVER

Commissioners Rd.

WALLY WORLD

TOURIST INFO

WESTMINSTER PONDS

Exeter Rd.

LONDON

Take a Hike: Next to the tourist information centre on Wellington Road, Westminster Ponds offers nature and hiking trails around kettle lakes, the predominant geological feature of this area. These lakes were formed when large ice-blocks, stranded by retreating glaciers, left large depressions, called kettles, that then filled with water.

Great bird-watching. No charge.
Further Afield: In downtown London, don't miss the historic Grand Theatre (restored and renovated), the Guy Lombardo Museum (dedicated to the famous New Year's Eve entertainer), Covent Garden (London's market since 1845), and the Children's Museum (a hands-on experience). The

University of Western Ontario is in the northwest area of the city.

#189
Highbury Avenue/ London

Highbury Avenue, a divided highway north of the 401, accesses the eastern areas of London. John Graves Simcoe had great expectations of this London. Although it never became the provincial capital, as Simcoe had hoped, it is today the centre of commerce and agriculture in Southwestern Ontario. The city is home base for such national companies as London Life Insurance, Canada Trust, and 3M.

➢ SOUTH

➢ NORTH

Dundas Street east (Highway 2), about 7 kilometres north of the 401, has services in both directions. Dundas Street runs west to downtown London and east to the airport.
Factory Outlet: Positive Identity Sportswear Factory Outlet, 455 Highbury Avenue, silk-screened and embroidered sportswear. Open Monday through Friday 10 A.M. to

5 P.M., Saturday 9 A.M. to 2 P.M., 519-452-1790.
Take a Hike: Turn off at the first exit, Bradley Avenue, and continue west to the first street, Pond Mills Road. This eastern area of Westminster Ponds connects with the park accessed from Wellington Road (see IC #186). More kettle lakes, picnic tables and trails. No charge.
Fair Days: Events are scheduled year-round at the Western Fairgrounds, but the really big show, the Western Fair, happens only once a year. The fair runs for 10 days in September, beginning the Friday after Labour Day. Take Highbury Avenue north and turn west on Dundas Street East, (8.5 kilometres from the 401), 519-438-7203.

#194
Highway 100/London

Highway 100 does not extend south of Highway 401. To the north it accesses a business and industrial area and the airport.

➢ NORTH

Further Afield: Fanshawe Conservation Area is about 14 kilometres north of the 401, via Highway 100, Oxford Street and Clarke Side Road. Fanshawe Pioneer Village is 3 kilometres farther north.

#195
Highway 74/
Nilestown Road/Nilestown

In Southwestern Ontario, many exits lead to fields of corn and herds of Holsteins. It's no mystery why this area is known as the breadbasket of Ontario.

➤ SOUTH
Services:

Husky Service Centre, open 24 hours.

➤ NORTH

Nilestown (population 84), a four-corner village, is 2.5 kilometres north of the 401.

On the Road Again: Follow County Road 29 east to Dorchester and return to the 401 at IC #199. See IC #199 for a great picnic spot near the millpond in Dorchester.

Husky Flag

One lasted only 12 hours. Some keep flying for months. The flags, measuring 20 feet (6 m) by 40 feet (12 m), are the largest privately flown flags in the country and they fly at 45 Husky Car/Truck Centres from as far north as Watson Lake, Yukon, east to Ontario.

By the laws of physics, that many square feet of fabric aloft at the end of a flagpole more than 100 feet (30 m) high take quite a beating. Simple rips are mended, but fading and tattering demand replacement. To continually show the colours, most centres keep a spare handy. Husky's head office estimates that 25 new flags a year are purchased to maintain stock.

Small planes approaching Windsor airport have been known to use the flag flying at the nearby centre at IC #014 as a windsock. At the same centre, during a bad storm in the winter of 1981–82, a motorist who became lost in a total whiteout could hear the flag snapping and followed the sound to safety. He figures it saved his life.

Husky has been flying the big flags for as long as the company has been in Canada, about 75 years. Look for them on Highway 401 at IC #014, IC #195 and IC #632.

#199
Dorchester Road/
Dorchester

Dorchester Road leads past tobacco kilns to Dorchester (population 2,750).

➤ SOUTH
Services:

Fifth Wheel Truck Stop, open 24 hours.

➤ NORTH
Services: In Dorchester, 4 kilometres

Off the Beaten Track: Hearthside Crafts is a small shop located in the miller's former stables at the corner of Mill Road and County Road 29 (Hamilton Road). Look for the big sign on the silo on the western edge of town. The miller's impressive stone house stands on the hill across the road. As was typical in many early Ontario settlements, the river here was dammed to produce power

for a sawmill, and then later, a flour mill. There is a lovely picnic spot beside the millpond. You can take the footbridge over the river and investigate the trail down the other side.

#203
Highway 73/Aylmer

Highway 73 leads south to Aylmer (21 kilometres) and eventually to Port Bruce on Lake Erie (36 kilometres).

➤ SOUTH

Off the Beaten Track: The town of Mossley (population 110) is 2 kilometres south on Highway 73. You can't miss the old general store—there is only one. Tall, narrow double doors open to a store stocked with 1990s packaged merchandise in among the 1890s fixtures. A weighty and elaborate manual cash-register rings up sales. Plans are afoot to convert the original post-office area into a boutique. The ice-cream cones are generously scooped.

➤ NORTH

On the Road Again: To the north, tobacco kilns and greenhouses line County Road 29 between IC #203 and IC #208.

#208
Putnam Road/ Middlesex Road 30/ Avon/Putnam

This is another one of those exits that leads the traveller to rural Ontario.

➢ SOUTH

➢ NORTH
Services: In Putnam, 1 kilometre

#216
Culloden Road/Oxford Road 10/Ingersoll

Culloden Road is on the western edge of the town of Ingersoll (population 8,900). The construction of the 401 opened up rural Ontario to industrial development by providing efficient access to markets across Ontario and into the United States. The CAMI plant on former pasture-land just north of the 401 produces automobiles for General Motors and Suzuki.

➢ SOUTH

➢ NORTH
Services:

 Travelodge

Other services in downtown Ingersoll, 3 kilometres. See IC #218.
Antiques: Any light fixture missing a piece can probably be made whole again at Shoults Antique Lighting, 345 King Street West. Overhead fixtures, table lamps, wall sconces—if it is antique and it sheds light on the subject, you can find it here. On a large wall-map of Ingersoll, proprietor Kent Shoults records his research of Ingersoll's past. At each street address, he pins a strip of paper recording the name of the business and its years of operation. He has been working on this project since 1970 and he expects it may take a few more years to complete. Open daily 7 A.M. to 9 P.M., 519-485-1440.
Factory Outlet: Underwood Shoes Ltd., 345 Ingersoll Street (across from the CAMI plant); Brooks, Kodiaks and Durango boots; open Monday to Friday 8 A.M. to 5 P.M.; Saturday 9 A.M. to 4 P.M., 519-485-1975.
On the Road Again: Continue through Ingersoll and return to the 401 via Highway 19, IC #218.

#218
Highway 19/Ingersoll/ Tillsonburg

Ingersoll is named for an early settler, Thomas Ingersoll, the father of Laura Secord. Both father and daughter were long gone before their names became associated with foodstuffs—Ingersoll with cheese and Secord with chocolates. Although credit is often given to James Harris of Elmhurst for establishing the cheddar cheese industry in Canada, the village of Salford, south of the 401, claims that local settlers Lydia Ranney and her husband, Hiram, were the real founders of the industry. Check out the museums in each town and make your own decision.

Ingersoll is 3 kilometres north of the 401. Tillsonburg is beyond our reach, 23 kilometres south.

➤ SOUTH
Services:

In Salford

Say Cheese: The Village Cheese Mill in Salford, 4.5 kilometres south, sells cheese and gift items in the store at the front. In the back room, the Salford Heritage Museum displays local artefacts documenting the area's history, its role in the development of the cheddar cheese industry, and the life and times of its most famous citizen, evangelist Amy Semple McPherson. The store and museum are open Monday through Saturday 10 A.M. to 5:30 P.M., 519-485-0600. McPherson's grave and

Tobacco Kilns

Much of the year an air of inactivity surrounds the big green sheds, and they look a bit like modest summer homes closed up for the season. But in spite of the success of the no-smoking lobby, the tobacco industry continues in Southwestern Ontario. While some former tobacco farmers are now growing ginseng and others are cultivating peanuts, many continue to grow tobacco.

When the crop is harvested, small bunches of tobacco leaves are tied together and these bunches are then tied on tobacco sticks. The sticks of tobacco leaves are moved into the kiln through the large openings; the doors on the openings are then closed and, with a fire heating the kiln to just the right temperature, the leaves are left to cure.

Although the heart of tobacco country is south of Highway 401, closer to Delhi and Tillsonburg, fields of tobacco and tobacco kilns can be seen in the area east of London around Dorchester and Nilestown (IC #195).

monument are located in the Harris Street Cemetery on the west side of Highway 19 just below the 401.

➤ NORTH
Services:

In Ingersoll

The Clog & Thistle, 189 Thames Street South, advertises casual fine dining and a second-floor gift shop in the 1832 Smith House. Open Monday and Tuesday 11 A.M. to 4 P.M.; Wednesday through Sunday 11 A.M. to 9 P.M., 519-425-0900.

Hospital: Alexandra Hospital, 20 Noxon, 519-485-1700.

Newspaper: *Ingersoll Times*, published weekly on Wednesdays.

Tourist Information: At the museum complex. Same hours (see below).

To Market: A flea and farmers' market operates year-round on Thursday 10 A.M. to 8 P.M., downtown on Thames Street South.

Roll Back the Clock: Directly off the 401, Elmhurst, the elaborate

Victorian villa built in 1871 by James Harris, son-in-law of Lydia Ranney, is a symbol of the success of Canadian cheddar. Harris, the Ranneys, and other area cheese-makers pooled their resources in 1866 and converted 35 tons of milk into a 7,300-pound (3,315 kg) cheese to display at the New York State Fair. Following its display at the fair, the cheese toured Canada and England, promoting Oxford County cheddar. Obviously the promotion was a success. Now called the Elm Hurst Inn, the house that cheese built offers accommodation, fine dining and a gift shop, 519-485-5321.

Step Back in Time: In a museum complex at the south of town on Highway 19, the Community Museum, the Agricultural Museum & Blacksmith Shop, the Cheese Factory Museum and the Sports Hall of Fame are open mid-May to the end of June and Labour Day to Thanksgiving, weekends only, 1 P.M. to 5 P.M.; July and August, daily 10 A.M. to 6 P.M. Donations accepted.

On the Road Again: If you need a rural "fix," take County Road 12 east off Highway 19 south to Foldens and return to the 401 at IC #222, or continue past Sweaburg (don't miss Jakeman's and Trillium Woods, described in IC #230) and return via IC #230. Or from Ingersoll, take County Road 9 past the lime quarries of Beachville (see IC #230) and return to the 401 at one of the Woodstock interchanges.

#222
Oxford Road 6/
Foldens/Embro

Take this exit to see the countryside.

➢ SOUTH

➢ NORTH
Services: In Beachville

Off the Beaten Track: What's in a name? Beachville, the Lime Capital of Canada, has neither beaches nor limes. It was named after an early grist-mill owner, Andrew Beach, and it does have some of the largest lime quarries in Canada. Ninety-five percent of the cement used in the construction of the CN Tower in Toronto came from these quarries. A far more important bit of trivia for baseball fans is the claim of the Beachville District Museum that the first recorded baseball game in North America was played in a Beachville pasture on June 4, 1838.

It is all documented in the museum. Take County Road 6 north from the 401 to County Road 9 and turn right. Open Wednesday, Thursday and Friday from 9:30 A.M. to 4:30 P.M. and Sunday from 12:30 P.M., or by appointment. Admission charge, 519-423-6497.

Tourist Information: Available at the museum. Same hours.

On the Road Again: Continue east into Woodstock on County Road 9 and return to the 401 at IC #230 or IC #232. Eastbound travellers interested in the spring attractions of IC #230 should take this exit south to Foldens and continue east to Sweaburg on County Road 12.

Baseball Beginnings

In a letter to *Sporting Life* magazine in 1886, Dr. Adam E. Ford, physician and former resident of Beachville, described a local ball game played on June 4, 1838, King George IV's birthday. The day had been declared a national holiday in Canada to celebrate the government's success in quelling the rebellion of the previous year. According to the Beachville Museum, Dr. Ford's careful documentation of the Beachville game, its rules and its participants stands as the first recorded baseball game played in North America, one year before the more famous Cooperstown game in 1839.

The rules varied just a bit from the game we know today. Bases were called "byes" and there were four, not three. To get from one base to the next, the runner could detour into the field to avoid "plugging." A runner between bases who was plugged, that is, hit by the ball, was out. A "knocker" was a batter, a "tick" was a foul caught by the catcher, and home plate was known as the "knocker's stone."

#230
Sweaburg Road/
Oxford Road 12/
Sweaburg/Woodstock

Sweaburg Road/Oxford Road 12 leads north into Woodstock (one of two exits to Woodstock) and to the south doubles back and runs west and parallel to the 401. Just beyond the village of Sweaburg, two truly Canadian attractions are worth a spring visit.

➤ SOUTH

Services: In Sweaburg, 3.5 kilometres

Clearly Canadian: Continue west through Sweaburg for 1.5 kilometres and take the gravel road to the right. In the original 1855 Sweaburg General Store and Post Office, the Jakeman family sells Jakeman maple products (syrup, candies), gifts and Aunt Ina's jams and relishes. These days, the sap is collected by pipeline and boiled down by oil-fired evaporators, a dramatic change from the pioneer Jakemans' time when sap was collected in wooden buckets and evaporated over an open wood-fire. Open year-round, Monday through Saturday 9 A.M. to 5 P.M. March, April, May, November and December, Sunday 10 A.M. to 4 P.M. On weekends, 10 A.M. to 4 P.M. from March to mid-April, pancakes and fresh syrup are served in the Pancake House, 519-539-1366.

Season's Best: In Trillium Woods Provincial Nature Reserve, directly across the road from Jakeman's, Ontario's provincial flower, the trillium, blooms in profusion in late April and May. Normally three white petals alternate with three green sepals, but here it is not unusual to find flower colour, size, and even shape aberrations. Green pigmentation in the white petals is not uncommon. Stay on the paths and look, but don't pick! No facilities. No charge.

Off the Beaten Track: Continue north on the gravel road and look to your left. The long oblong hill is a drumlin, a glacial hill composed of loam deposited by a retreating glacier. Drumlins are a common geological feature in parts of Southern Ontario.

➤ NORTH
Services:

All services in Woodstock, 3 kilometres.

Roll Back the Clock: County Road 12 becomes Mill Street in Woodstock. Turn east from it onto Dundas Street and then turn north on Vansittart Avenue. Behind the wide tree-lined boulevards of Vansittart Avenue are well-kept, turreted, Victorian residences—an architectural heritage preserved from Woodstock's turn-of-the-century prosperity. Criss-cross

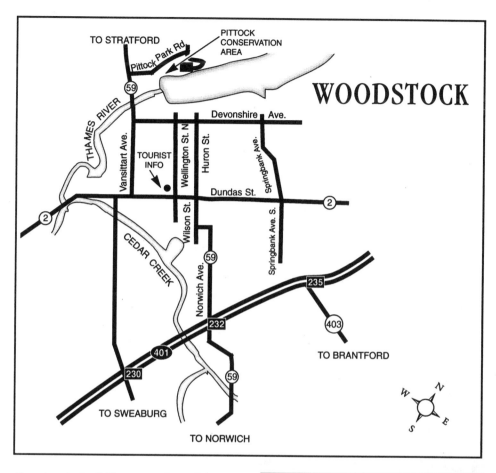

TO STRATFORD

PITTOCK CONSERVATION AREA

Pittock Park Rd

THAMES RIVER

59

Vansittart Ave.

TOURIST INFO

Wellington St. N

Huron St.

Devonshire Ave.

Springbank Ave.

Dundas St.

2

Springbank Ave. S.

Wilson St.

59

Norwich Ave.

CEDAR CREEK

235

232

403

401

230

59

TO BRANTFORD

TO SWEABURG

TO NORWICH

WOODSTOCK

2

the streets to fully appreciate the impressive stone and brick work.

To Market: The Woodstock Flea and Farmers' Market, a small market at Mill Street and Main Street, is open Saturday 7 A.M. to 4 P.M.

Picnic in the Park: Continue north on Vansittart Avenue and turn right at the sign for Pittock Conservation Area. Proceed another kilometre for a total of 6.5 kilometres from the 401. Swimming, picnic and boat facilities, fishing and hiking trails. Washrooms. Open May through October. Admission charge, 519-539-5088.

INTERCHANGE

#232
Highway 59/
Woodstock/Delhi

Highway 59 north is the main exit to downtown Woodstock (population 29,000). The city centre is about 3 kilometres from the 401. Delhi is 40 kilometres south.

Known as the dairy capital of Canada, Woodstock is the hub of a large agricultural area. Dairy farmers in fertile Oxford County depend for their success on prize-winning herds and they have singled out one Holstein matriarch for special recognition. On Dundas Street East near Springbank Avenue, a life-size statue honours Springbank Snow Countess, World Champion Lifetime Butterfat Producer.

➤ SOUTH

➤ NORTH

Services:

In Woodstock and on Highway 2 east and west, all services, including

Hospital: Woodstock General Hospital, 270 Riddell Street, 519-421-4211.

Newspaper: *Daily Sentinel-Review*

Radio Station: K104 FM 103.9

Tourist Information: At the Woodstock District Chamber of

Klondike Joe Boyle—Larger Than Life

Joe Boyle was born in 1867 in Toronto and raised in Woodstock. He was a restless and ruthless entrepreneur and a trouble-shooter whose event-filled life propelled him from one adventure to another around the world, behind enemy lines and into the hearts of the Romanian royal family.

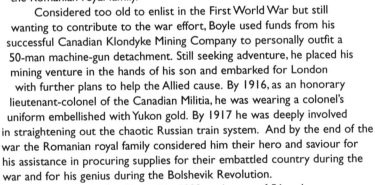

Considered too old to enlist in the First World War but still wanting to contribute to the war effort, Boyle used funds from his successful Canadian Klondyke Mining Company to personally outfit a 50-man machine-gun detachment. Still seeking adventure, he placed his mining venture in the hands of his son and embarked for London with further plans to help the Allied cause. By 1916, as an honorary lieutenant-colonel of the Canadian Militia, he was wearing a colonel's uniform embellished with Yukon gold. By 1917 he was deeply involved in straightening out the chaotic Russian train system. And by the end of the war the Romanian royal family considered him their hero and saviour for his assistance in procuring supplies for their embattled country during the war and for his genius during the Bolshevik Revolution.

When Boyle died in England in 1923 at the age of 56 and was interred in the cemetery of St. James Church in Hampton Hill, Queen Marie of Romania, in acknowledgment of her country's deep affection for him, marked his grave site with a thousand-year-old stone cross. That cross, along with an urn and the Romanian ivy that grew on his English grave, now mark Joe Boyle's final resting place in the Presbyterian cemetery on Vansittart Avenue in Woodstock. The Woodstock Museum (IC #232) sells a publication, *In Praise of a Canadian Hero*, that details his remarkable story.

Commerce, 18 Wellington Street North, information is available year-round during business hours, Monday through Friday, 519-539-9411. An information kiosk next to the Countess's statue operates in July and August, daily 8 A.M. to 7 P.M.

To Market: A farmers' market takes place year-round at the Woodstock Fairgrounds, 875 Nellis Street, Saturday 7 A.M. to noon.

Say Cheese: The Dairy Capital Cheese Shoppe & Deli-Cafe, 474 Dundas Street, sells a large selection of cheeses and specialty foods and serves light meals and desserts, 519-537-7623.

Factory Outlet: Sunwear Factory Outlet, 97 Wilson Street, sportswear, underwear and socks. Open Monday through Thursday 9:30 A.M. to 6 P.M.; Friday 9:30 A.M. to 9 P.M.; Saturday 9:30 A.M. to 5 P.M., 519-539-2195.

For Art's Sake: The Woodstock Art Gallery is housed in a 1913 neo-Georgian manse at 447 Hunter Street. Open Tuesday through Friday 11 A.M. to 5 P.M.; Saturday 10 A.M. to 5 P.M.; Sunday 1:30 P.M. to 5 P.M. No charge, 519-539-6761.

Step Back in Time: The Woodstock Museum, in the restored 1889 town hall at 466 Dundas Street, displays Oxford County memorabilia. Open year-round Tuesday through Saturday 10 A.M. to 5 P.M. Also, July and August, Sunday 1 P.M. to 5 P.M.; Monday 10 A.M. to 5 P.M. Donations accepted, 519-537-8411.

Fair Days: Each year, beginning on the Wednesday of the third full week in August, the Woodstock Fair celebrates the area's rural roots. The fairgrounds are located at 875 Nellis Street.

On the Road Again: Highway 2 east leads back to the 401 at IC #236 or IC #238.

INTERCHANGE

#235
Highway 403/Brantford

Highway 403 is a divided highway to Brantford, running only southeast from Woodstock.

The first exit on Highway 403 is Highway 53. A return to the 401 is possible from Eastwood.

INTERCHANGE

#236
Towerline Road/
Oxford Road 15/
Woodstock

Take this exit north to Highway 2 and Woodstock, and south to more of rural Ontario.

➤ **SOUTH**

➤ **NORTH**

Services: For services on Highway 2, see IC #238.

#238
Highway 2/Eastwood/ Woodstock/Paris

Highway 2 leads west into Woodstock and east to the small community of Eastwood at the junction of Highways 2 and 53 (3 kilometres). For Woodstock information see IC #232.

➤ EAST
Services:

➤ WEST
Services:

Blandford Square Mall

Other services close to Woodstock include

Burger King McDonald's Tim Hortons.

Sunoco

OPP: Just off the 401, 519-539-9811.

On the Road Again: What stands 5 or 6 feet (1.8 m) tall and lays 5-inch (13 cm), dark green, avocado-like eggs? Drop in at Hillcrest Emu Farm and see for yourself. Take County Road 4 east from Highway 2 for 5.5 kilometres and turn right at Ray's Car Sales. At the third farm on the west side of the road (about 1 kilometre north) the big birds can easily be seen in their summer outdoor pens. Visitors are welcome to tour the facilities. Spring, summer and fall, daily 10 A.M. to 8 P.M.; winter, 10 A.M. to 4 P.M.; 519-469-3217. Continue on County Road 4 through Innerkip and return to the 401 at IC #250.

#250
Drumbo Road/ Oxford Road 29/ Drumbo/Innerkip

Exit in either direction and you will come to a small village—Drumbo, 3 kilometres east (population 530) and Innerkip, 8.5 kilometres west (population 830).

➤ EAST
Services: In Drumbo

So many place names in Canada come from the homelands of the pioneers, and Drumbo, named after Drumbo, Ireland, is no exception.

Off the Beaten Track: Take County Road 3 north from Drumbo for 1.5 kilometres. Turn right on Wolverton Road and continue into the village of Wolverton. Wolverton Hall, a private residence not open to the public, is on the first street to the left. It is a fine example of a large, well-maintained brick house of the 1850s.

➤ WEST

Services: None till Innerkip

Picnic in the Park: Formerly a quarry, Trout Lake is a favourite spot for swimmers and scuba divers. This private park on the western edge of Innerkip has picnic facilities and campsites. Admission charge, 519-469-3363.

Take a Hike: Keep your eyes peeled about 3 kilometres north of the 401 for the only sign indicating the right turn for Chesney Conservation Area. A narrow dirt road leads into a delightful reserve with picnic tables, outdoor washrooms and marked trails. No charge.

#268
Waterloo Road 97/
Plattsville/Ayr

➤ EAST

Services:

Take a Hike: The F.W.R. Dickson Wilderness Area pushes the 10-minute limit, and Pinehurst Lake Conservation Area is a couple of minutes further south. Follow County Road 97 for 3 kilometres to County Road 47 and turn right. Follow County Road 47 until it meets County Road 49 (5.3 kilometres). Turn left at County Road 49 and after a short distance turn right onto County Road 75. At Brant Waterloo Road (about 1 kilometre), turn right again. F.W.R. Dickson Wilderness Area is on the right, just past the campground. Picnic tables, hiking trails, boardwalks. No charge.

For a more developed recreation area, return to County Road 75 and turn right. Continue south on what becomes Highway 24A for 1.5 kilometres. At Pinehurst Lake Conservation Area, the spring-fed kettle lake offers swimming, fishing, and boating. There is also a children's

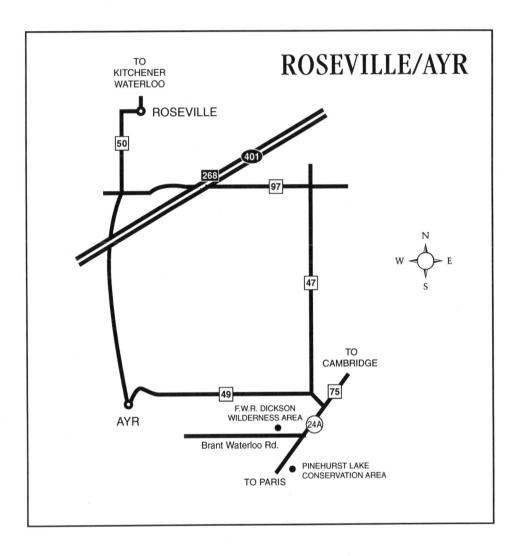

ROSEVILLE/AYR

TO KITCHENER WATERLOO

ROSEVILLE

50

401

268

97

47

N
W · E
S

TO CAMBRIDGE

49

75

F.W.R. DICKSON WILDERNESS AREA

AYR

24A

Brant Waterloo Rd.

PINEHURST LAKE CONSERVATION AREA

TO PARIS

---

playground and in winter cross-country ski trails. Admission charge, 519-442-4721.

➢ WEST

Roll Back the Clock: Drive west on County Road 8 to the intersection with County Road 50 (2.5 kilometres).

Before turning left on County Road 50 to the village of Ayr, notice the sign on the northeast corner marking the site of a former community, Black Horse Corner. Apparently the settlement was named for an early innkeeper's favourite black Clydesdales. Follow County Road 50 south for 3.5 kilometres to Ayr (population 1,300). Here, beside the millpond in the centre of town, enjoy a picnic or drop into one of the restaurants—Bucky's Coffee Shop where the coffee pot is always on, or the Mill Pond Restaurant for all-day breakfasts and Fondue Fridays. In the long, low, brick building in the centre of town, the John Watson Manufacturing Company began producing cast-iron pots in 1847. It moved on to the invention and production of agricultural implements, contributed to the war effort by producing push trucks, and supplied foundry items to the railways. It's reported that the town's cast-iron hitching posts and lamp standards came from the foundry.

Antiques: Sawmill Antiques of Roseville (north on County Road 50 from County Road 8) is open Wednesday through Friday 10 A.M. to 4 P.M.; Saturday, Sunday and holidays, noon to 6 P.M., 519-696-2911. Roseville also has a general store and restaurant.

On the Road Again: North of Roseville, County Road 50 intersects County Road 12. Detour west on County Road 12 to New Dundee (3.5 kilometres). In an 1887 building at 169 Front Street is an old-fashioned store, the Tea Room and Emporium. Closed Monday, 519-696-2223. Kalitas Coiffures and Antiques is right next door. Return east on County Road 12 to Kitchener and return to the 401 at IC #275.

From Dickson Wilderness Area or Pinehurst Lake Conservation Area, follow County Road 75 northeast to Cambridge and return to the 401 via either Highway 8 or Highway 24.

#275
Fountain Street/ Homer Watson Boulevard/ Cambridge/ Kitchener

In 1994, the provincial and federal governments declared the Grand River a Heritage River, recognizing its outstanding heritage and recreational resources. Have a look at the Grand at either IC #275 or IC #278.

➤ SOUTH

Off the Beaten Track: Sheaves Tower, one of the world's smallest hydro projects, was built in 1876 to provide additional power for Blair Mills. From Fountain Street, turn right onto Blair Road, right at Meadowcreek Lane and right again at Old Mill Road. The tower is located on private property across the road from the mill but can easily be seen from the road.

Roll Back the Clock: In the town of Blair, you will find 19th-century buildings both modest and grand. The white clapboard house on the main street, across from the Garden Gate (a gift shop), was a general store built in 1882. Note its unusual corner door. Langdon Hall (south on Blair Road and west on Langdon

Drive), a country inn built in 1898 as a sumptuous summer home, today offers Grand hospitality.

Picnic in the Park: For a quiet moment beside the Grand, pull into the parking area of Moyers Blair Landing, south on Fountain Street. Parking, picnic facilities and a great river view. No charge.

➤ NORTH

Services:

 Sunoco

Step Back in Time: At Doon Heritage Crossroads, a living-history village 3 kilometres north on Homer Watson Boulevard (at the corner of Huron Road), visitors get a glimpse of an early 20th-century community adapting to a radically changing lifestyle as automobiles, electricity and telephones become a part of everyday life. Open May through September, daily 10 A.M. to 4:30 P.M.; October through December, Monday through Friday 10 A.M. to 4:30 P.M. Gift shop and picnic area. Admission charge, 519-748-1914.

For Art's Sake: The Homer Watson House and Gallery was once the home and studio of Homer Watson, Canada's pre-eminent landscape painter of the late 19th and early 20th centuries. Watson's art and the works of contemporary artists are displayed here. To reach the

museum and gallery at 1754 Old Mill Road, continue east on Huron Road from the Doon Heritage Crossroads or follow the signs at Conestoga College Boulevard. Open April through December, Tuesday through Sunday noon to 4:30 P.M., and holiday Mondays, 519-748-4377. Donations accepted. At the museum pick up a map of the Doon Presbyterian Cemetery (between the crossroads and the museum). Many early Doon residents, including Homer Watson, are buried here. An excellent guide to the area, "Waterloo–Wellington Driving Tour," may be purchased at the museum.

On the Road Again: Homer Watson Boulevard continues south of the 401 as Fountain Street and more or less parallels Highway 401 to the old town of Preston, now part of Cambridge. Blair Road follows the Grand River south to the city centre of Cambridge, the former town of Galt. Return to the 401 via any of the Cambridge interchanges.

INTERCHANGE

#278
Highway 8/
Cambridge/Kitchener/
Waterloo

Eastbound travellers exit directly onto old Highway 8 to either Cambridge or Kitchener. Westbound travellers to Kitchener must choose

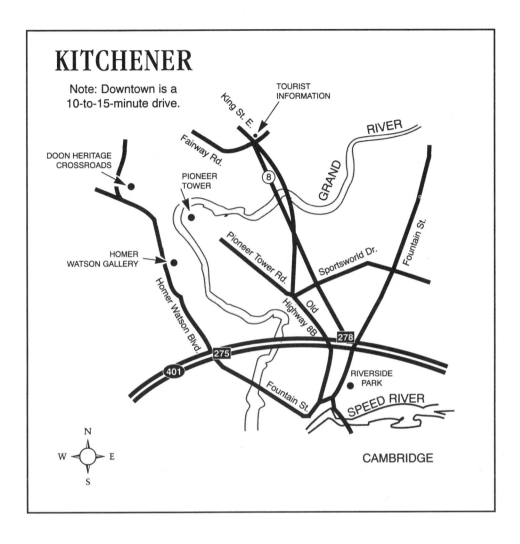

KITCHENER

Note: Downtown is a
10-to-15-minute drive.

either Highway 8 Kitchener/
Waterloo, a controlled-access route
to downtown, or Highway 8/King
Street, the old highway. For immediate services, choose the old highway or exit at the first or second
interchange of the parkway.
Depending on the route downtown,
Kitchener is a 10-to-15-minute drive
from the 401. Also, see IC #282 for
Cambridge.

> SOUTH

Services:

  Tim Hortons.

   Sunoco

Hospital: Cambridge Memorial
Hospital, 700 Coronation Street,
519-621-2330.

Tourist Information: The Cambridge Chamber of Commerce at 531 King Street East is open year-round Monday through Friday 9 A.M. to 5 P.M., 1-800-749-7560. See IC #282 for a second seasonal tourist information centre.

Roll Back the Clock: In 1973, the City of Cambridge was created by the amalgamation of Galt, Preston and Hespeler. Each town began and developed beside a powerful river—Hespeler and Preston on the Speed River, and Galt on the Grand. Visitors flocked to Preston at the turn of the century to bathe in the healing waters of the nearby sulphur springs. The massive five-storey hotel at the top of King Street, the largest of Preston's former health resort hotels, is currently being renovated as a retirement home.

Factory Outlets: Cambridge boasts a great many factory outlets—some are authentic, some are not. Ask for the factory-outlet guide at the tourist information centre. One outlet close to the 401 is Dover Flour Mills, 140 King Street West, where you can buy bakery flour, wheat germ and yeast. Open Monday through Friday 8:30 A.M. to 5 P.M., 519-653-6267. See IC #282 and IC #284 for other factory outlets.

Picnic in the Park: Of Cambridge's 37 parks, Riverside Park on the Speed River is the closest to the 401. Playground, animal farm, bicycle paths, walkways. Located between Fountain Street East and King Street. No charge.

➤ NORTH

Services:

  Tim Hortons. *McDonald's*

  PETRO-CANADA® Sunoco

More services at Fairway Road.

Hospital: Kitchener–Waterloo Hospital, 835 King Street West, 519-742-3611.

Newspaper: *Kitchener–Waterloo Record*, daily.

Radio Stations: CFCA FM 105.3, CHYM FM 96.7, CKGL AM 570, CKGL AM 1090

Tourist Information: Kitchener Chamber of Commerce, 2848 King Street East, 1-800-265-6959. Open Monday through Friday 9 A.M. to 5 P.M. all year; during June, July and August, also Saturday and Sunday from 10 A.M. to 4 P.M.

Play Awhile: Sportsworld, a 30-acre (12 ha) activity park with water slides, a wave pool and miniature golf is less than 2 kilometres north on Highway 8 at 100 Sportsworld Drive. Open daily year-round. Activities and hours vary seasonally. Moose Winooski's (a restaurant, of course!) is open weekdays 11 A.M. to 1 A.M., weekends noon to 1 A.M., 519-653-4442.

Off the Beaten Track: From old Highway 8, turn left opposite Sportsworld Drive, and follow Pioneer Road for 2 kilometres to the sign for Dawn-Glo Village. Turn left again. Beside the farm, which offers wagon rides and hourly trail riding, in a small park above the Grand Valley, a stone tower commemorates the 1800 arrival of the first Mennonite settlers to the area. Enjoy a Grand view from the top of the tower. The park is open year-round; the tower from mid-June to Labour Day, Tuesday through Sunday 10 A.M. to 5 P.M. No charge.

Factory Outlets: Ask for a complete list of factory outlets at the tourist information centre. *Arrow Factory Retail Outlet,* 112 Benton Street, men's and ladies' shirts and sweaters, Monday through Saturday 9 A.M. to 5 P.M.; Sunday noon to 4 P.M. 519-743-8211. *Bonnie Stuart Shoes,* 141 Whitney Place, children's shoes, Thursday 4 P.M. to 8 P.M.; Saturday 9 A.M. to 3 P.M., 519-578-8880.

Special Events: Oktoberfest begins in Kitchener the Friday before Thanksgiving in October and continues for another 8 days. This event is North America's largest Bavarian festival. The parade on Thanksgiving Monday begins early in the morning and continues till midday, 519-570-HANS.

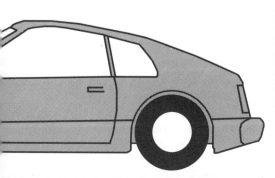

INTERCHANGE

#282
Highway 24/
Hespeler Road/
Cambridge
★

Highway 24 connects the three former towns now amalgamated into the City of Cambridge (population 92,000). Hespeler is to the north. Galt is south of the intersection of Highway 8 and Highway 24 (4 kilometres) and Preston is west via Eagle Street.

➤ SOUTH
Services:

Knob Hill Farms Food Terminal, south on Hespeler Road, claims to be the world's largest retail food outlet. The store covers almost 8 acres (3.2 ha), has 49 checkouts, more than a mile of refrigeration and coolers, a produce department over an acre in size, and sits on a 25-acre (10 ha) site with parking for 1,000 cars. Open daily.

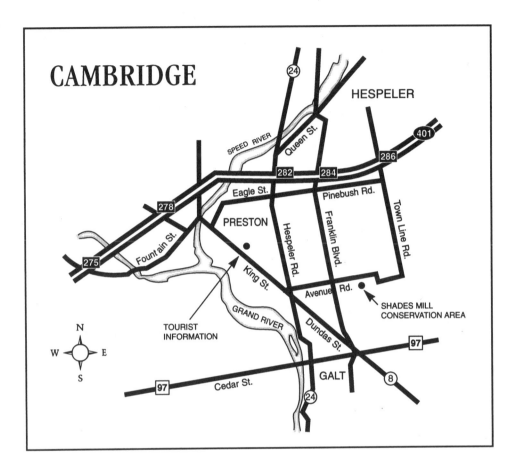

Newspapers: *Cambridge Reporter*, daily. *Cambridge Times*, Wednesday and Sunday.

Radio Stations: CIAM AM 96

Tourist Information: On Highway 24 south at the PetroCanada station. From Victoria Day to Labour Day, daily 9 A.M. to 7 P.M. See also IC #278.

To Market: At the corner of Dickson and Ainslie Streets (south of the intersection of Highways 8 and 24), on Saturday mornings and summer Wednesday mornings, a farmers' market is held in a building built for that purpose in 1887.

Factory Outlets: *Vachon*, 623 Hespeler Road. Crackers, cookies, cakes. Open Wednesday through Friday, noon to 5 P.M.; Saturday 10 A.M. to 3 P.M., 519-621-7021. *Forsyth Factory Outlet*, 425 Hespeler Road, men's and ladies shirts, Penman sportswear, open Monday through Wednesday, and Saturday 10 A.M. to 6 P.M.; Thursday and Friday 10 A.M. to 8 P.M.; Sunday noon to 5 P.M., 519-740-6570. Also see IC #284 and IC #278.

Bargain Hunt: Grand River Flea Market at 261 Hespeler Road advertises "lots of stuff" for sale—

everything from junk to jewellery. Open Saturday and Sunday 9 A.M. to 5 P.M.

➤ NORTH

Services: Queen Street exit into old Hespeler

Factory Outlets: The mammoth mills beside the Speed River in Hespeler lend an air of authenticity to Hespeler's factory outlets. *Len's Mill Stores*, 215 Queen Street, clothing, fabric, yarns. Open Monday through Wednesday, and Saturday 10 A.M. to 5 P.M.; Thursday and Friday 10 A.M. to 9 P.M.; Sunday 12:30 P.M. to 4:30 P.M., 519-658-8182. *Cambridge Fibres Ltd.*, 215 Queen Street, yarns, pillow forms, craft supplies. Same hours as Len's, 519-658-8237. *Raine's Fabrics*, 211 Queen Street, fabrics, notions and trim, bridal accessories. Monday through Wednesday, and Saturday, 9 A.M. to 6 P.M.; Thursday and Friday 9 A.M. to 9 P.M.; Sunday 11 A.M. to 5 P.M., 519-658-4643.

Further Afield: Highway 24 meets Highway 8, 4 kilometres south of the 401. The old town of Galt, named for the Scottish novelist and explorer John Galt, is farther south and pushes our 10-minute limit from the 401. But the stonework in the town is superb. Pick up a walking-tour

booklet and discover the heritage buildings and parks along the Grand River or check out the following: Cambridge Mill Restaurant, 4 Parkhill Road West, 519-740-2900, open Tuesday through Sunday; Southworks Antiques, 64 Grand Avenue South, open Monday through Wednesday 10 A.M. to 6 P.M., Thursday and Friday till 7 P.M., Saturday 9 A.M. to 5 P.M., and Sunday 11 A.M. to 4 P.M.

INTERCHANGE

#284
Franklin Boulevard/ Cambridge

Franklin Boulevard is a relatively new exit off the 401 providing access to eastern Cambridge for eastbound travellers only. Since there is no exit from the 401 west to Franklin Boulevard, westbound travellers should access all of IC #284 from IC #282.

SOUTH

Services:

Factory Outlets: *The Cookie Store*, 46 Stafford Court (turn left just south of the 401), Colonial cookies, open

Monday through Saturday 10 A.M. to
4:30 P.M., 519-622-2611. *McCordick
Glove Inc.*, 75 Cowansview Road
(right at Lindsay Road), coveralls,
gloves and safety items. Open
Monday through Friday 8 A.M. to
4 P.M., Saturday 9 A.M. to 3 P.M.,
519-623-9710. *Cambridge Towel Mill
Outlet*, 450 Dobbie Drive (turn left
1.2 kilometres south at Clyde Road),
towels, kitchen and bathroom
accessories. Open Monday through
Thursday, and Saturday 9 A.M. to
5 P.M.; Friday till 9 P.M.; Sunday noon
to 4 P.M., 519-622-5542.

Picnic in the Park: Shade's Mill
Conservation Area is located south
on Franklin Avenue about 3 kilometres and east on Avenue Road
another half a kilometre. Swimming, boating, hiking, picnic and
playground facilities. Admission
charge. Open from May to mid-
October.

➤ NORTH
Services:

On the Road Again: There is no
return to the 401 eastbound from
Franklin Boulevard. To continue
east, follow Pinebush Road to the
intersection with Townline Road and
return to the 401 east at IC #286.

#286
Regional Road 33/ Townline Road/ Cambridge

Pinebush Road, the continuation
of Eagle Street from King Street/
Highway 8 in Cambridge, dead-ends
here.

➤ SOUTH
Services:

For the Old Marina Restaurant and
Gift Shoppe, turn left on County
Road 32 toward Puslinch Lake and
continue for about 2 kilometres to
McClintock Drive. Turn right. At this
lakefront family restaurant, diners
have a front-row view of the practice
sessions of the competitive water-
skiers who train here in the summer.
Open daily 11:30 A.M. to 9 P.M., till
midnight on Friday and Saturday,
519-658-0367.

➤ NORTH

INTERCHANGE

#295
Highway 6 North/ Hanlon Expressway/ Guelph

Highway 6 North/Hanlon Express-way runs only north to the city of Guelph. Downtown Guelph (population 93,000) is a 13-kilometre, 15-minute drive from the 401 on this divided and controlled-access expressway.

➤ NORTH

Radio Stations: CIMJ FM 106.1, CJOY AM 1460

For the Birds: At the Kortright Waterfowl Park, approximately 1,000 captive birds, representing more than 90 different species of ducks, geese and swans from around the world, are joined by wild ducks and geese who make this traditional winter refuge their home. The land is owned by the Grand River Conservation Authority, and the park is operated by the Niska Wildlife Foundation, a private, non-profit organization committed to the preservation of our environment. Niska is a Swampy Cree word meaning grey or Canada goose. The park is open from March 1 to October 31, Saturday, Sunday and holidays 10 A.M. to 5 P.M. Turn left at Kortright Road 8.5 kilometres north of the 401 and make a right on Niska Road after a few hundred metres. A century farm, the Hanlon Farm, is visible on the right.

Waves of Rocks

At some time in the history of the Earth's surface, pressure from opposite sides forced too much rock into too little space and the surface buckled and folded. The result looks like waves of rocks. Recent widening of Highway 401 has exposed some great examples of these waves between IC #282 and IC #312. And because the anticline, the crest of the wave, and the syncline, the trough of the wave, rarely exist singly, if you miss the first one, keep watching.

Further Afield: John Galt founded Guelph in 1827 and gave the city the ancient family name of Britain's reigning monarch, George IV. Guelph continues to call itself the Royal City. A visit to the city should include a visit to the birthplace of John McCrae, author of the world-famous poem that begins "In Flanders fields the poppies blow Between the crosses, row on row." McCrae wrote the poem while he was a lieutenant-colonel with the Canadian Army Medical Corps during the First World War. The small red poppies that grow wild in much of Europe and inspired the poem have become the universal symbol of remembrance. McCrae died in France in 1918. The McCrae House, operated as a museum, is at 108 Water Street.

INTERCHANGE

#299
Highway 6 South/ Hamilton/Brock Road/ Aberfoyle/ Guelph

This is the long route into Guelph. Don't confuse Guelph with Galt. One town was founded by John Galt and the other one named for him.

➤ SOUTH
Services:

In the tiny village of Morristown, the heritage buildings along the main street provide the perfect setting for gift and antique shops and restaurants. On the menu at the Tea Room are teas, desserts and light meals. Open Tuesday through Sunday, 11 A.M. to 5 P.M. weekdays, open until 6 P.M. weekends, 519-823-0564.
Picnic in the Park: A small park on the west side of Highway 6 at the south of town offers benches and tables for a picnic.

➤ NORTH
Services:

The imposing stone grist-mill in the crossroads community of Aberfoyle was built in 1859 by Scotsman George McLean. It is now home to the Aberfoyle Mill Restaurant, which serves upscale lunches and dinners daily, 519-763-1070.

Antiques: The Aberfoyle Antique Market is billed as "Canada's Largest and Oldest Outdoor Antique Market." Every Sunday from 9 A.M. to 5 P.M., May to October, 100-plus dealers (some permanent and some casual) set up their wares, 519-763-1077.

On the Road Again: Alternate routes tend to involve to-ing and fro-ing, so it is probably simpler to backtrack to the 401.

INTERCHANGE

#312
Guelph Line/
Campbellville

Along the 401 from IC #312 to IC #320, a towering rocky ridge dominates the landscape. The Niagara Escarpment stretches for 725 kilometres from Niagara to Tobermory, and along its length, wilderness areas offer innumerable recreational opportunities. In 1990, UNESCO declared the Niagara Escarpment a World Biosphere Reserve. This designation places the Niagara Escarpment among such other internationally recognized ecosystems as the Galapagos Islands and the Serengeti Plain. Call the Halton Regional Conservation Authority at 905-336-1158 weekdays for programs and activities offered at the five conservation areas within easy reach of the 401. Also see IC #320.

➤ **SOUTH**

Services: In Campbellville

Antiques: Antique shops abound in Campbellville. The Stone House of Campbellville, 2 kilometres from the 401 and just beyond the town of Campbellville on Guelph Line, has on hand year-round hundreds of stained-glass windows from England and Scotland. Note the late-1800s stone farmhouse from which the shop takes its name, 905-854-2152 or 854-0261.

Take a Hike: The Mountsberg Conservation Area is located just north of Campbellville Road 9 and Milborough Line. The area offers hiking trails, picnic facilities, a maple-sugar bush, a skating pond, and a raptor (birds of prey) centre with bird hospital facilities, a flyway amphitheatre, and a raptor walkway. Open daily. Programs on weekends and holidays. Admission charge. 905-854-2276 (weekends).

At Crawford Lake Conservation Area, 4 kilometres south on Guelph Line, interpretive stations along an elevated boardwalk circling the lake explain its ecological uniqueness. The lake is so deep for its surface area that weather fluctuations never disturb the lower layers and the unruffled sediment records the passing years of life around the lake. The reconstructed 15th-century Iroquois village is based on information recovered from these layers of sediment. Hiking trails, displays and presentations, picnic facilities and washrooms. Open year-round daily, 10 A.M. to 4 P.M. Admission charge. 905-854-0234 (weekends).

➤ NORTH

Services:

 Sunoco

Off to the Races: Mohawk Raceway, directly north on Guelph Line, features Canada's best trotters and pacers in regular evening harness races. Dining room. Call 1-800-268-9967 for schedule. See page 65 for more on harness racing.

Off the Beaten Track: In the graveyard of St. John's Anglican Church on the corner of Guelph Line and Number 10 Sideroad, many headstones date to the mid-1800s. The stone church was rebuilt in 1870 to replace the original 1844 building.

Further Afield: For railway buffs, the Halton County Radial Railway Museum, 15 kilometres north on Guelph Line, is open in July and August, daily 10 A.M. to 5 P.M. For other seasons, phone for hours, 519-856-9802. Admission charge.

On the Road Again: For another Escarpment experience, take County Road 9 just north of the 401 and go

east for 4 kilometres to Hilton Falls Conservation Area. Enjoy mill ruins, hiking trails, beaver ponds and a falls—equally spectacular in summer or winter. Picnic facilities, washrooms. Open all year 8:30 A.M. to sunset. Admission charge. 905-854-0262 (weekends). From Hilton Falls continue east to Town Line. Turn south and pass under the 401 for the quickest route to the Ontario Agricultural Museum, Kelso Conservation Area and Halton Regional Museum, and Rattlesnake Point Conservation Area. (See IC #320.) Or stay on County Road 9 east to Highway 25 for a return to the 401. Westbound travellers may access Hilton Falls from Highway 25 north at IC #320.

INTERCHANGE

#320
Highway 25/Milton/ Halton Hills/ Acton

Highway 25 leads directly south to Milton (2.4 kilometres to Main Street) and north 17 kilometres to Acton. So inspired by the poetry of John Milton were the early settlers that in 1837 they named their town in his honour. Milton has grown from a grist-mill settlement tucked beneath the Niagara Escarpment on Sixteen Mile Creek to an agricultural hub of 33,000. Milton's prosperity is evident in the fine heritage buildings still standing on its tree-lined streets.

➤ SOUTH
Services:

Other services in Milton.
OPP: Highway 25 and Steeles Avenue West, 905-878-2307.
Hospital: Milton District Hospital, 30 Derry Road East, 905-878-2383.
Newspaper: *The Canadian Champion*, Wednesday and Friday.
Tourist Information: A year-round tourist office is open in the old train station on Highway 25 just south of the 401, September to June, Monday through Friday 9 A.M. to 5 P.M. and

---

Harness Racing

Harness racing has been a part of Ontario sporting life since the early 1800s when neighbour challenged neighbour along country roads and village streets. Over the years, the buggies became smaller, the horses more finely bred and the contests more formalized.

The number of half-mile training ovals easily spotted from the 401 affirms rural Ontario's continued fascination with the magic between horse, driver and cart. In harness racing, no pint-sized jockeys need apply. A driver perches on a next-to-nothing cart formally called a sulky—really just a seat with two wheels and two shafts—and drives a horse harnessed into the flimsy apparatus at breakneck speed around a banked and graded track covered in "stone dust." The sulkies used for training are called jogging carts; those used in actual races are racing bikes.

Standardbred horses either pace or trot, but not both. A pacer strides first with the right front and back legs at the same time and then with the left front and back legs. Hobbles restrict movement beyond that gait and prevent the horse from breaking stride. A trotter, in a more natural gait, strides with the right front and left back leg and then with the left front and right back. Either way, the horses storm around the track, legs flying, manes dishevelled, and ears bent to the wind, under the watchful eyes of owners whose hopes are pinned on the stopwatch.

Training ovals can be seen from Highway 401, 9 kilometres west of IC #509 (Brighton) on the north side, just west of IC #786 (Power Dam Road) on the north side, and on the south side just east of IC #208 (east of London). For anyone wishing to watch some harness racing and maybe even wager the odd dollar, there are a number of choices. Mohawk Raceway is directly off the 401 at IC #312, 1-800-268-9967. Other tracks within easy reach of the 401 are Kingston Park Raceway, 613-549-2314; Western Fair Raceway, 519-438-7203; Windsor Raceway 519-969-8311; Woodstock Raceway, 519-537-8212.

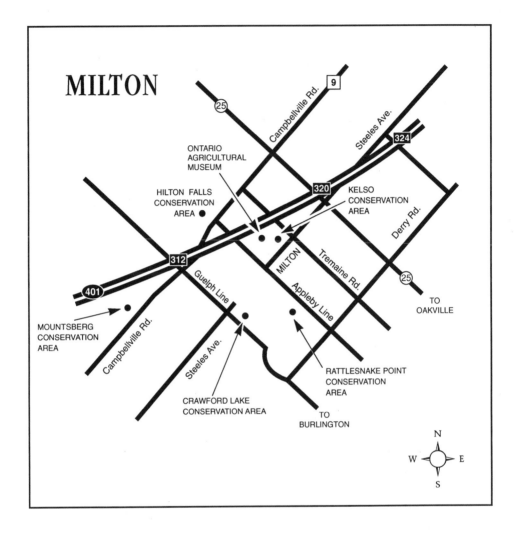

MILTON

ONTARIO
AGRICULTURAL
MUSEUM

HILTON FALLS
CONSERVATION
AREA ●

KELSO
CONSERVATION
AREA

Campbellville Rd.

Steeles Ave.

Tremaine Rd.

Derry Rd.

MILTON

Appleby Line

Guelph Line

MOUNTSBERG
CONSERVATION
AREA

Campbellville Rd.

Steeles Ave.

RATTLESNAKE POINT
CONSERVATION
AREA

CRAWFORD LAKE
CONSERVATION AREA

TO
BURLINGTON

TO
OAKVILLE

N
W ─◆─ E
S

the same hours daily during July and August, 905-878-0581.

To Market: On Saturday mornings from June to October a farmers' market is held on Main Street between James and Martin Streets.

Step Back in Time: The Ontario Agricultural Museum, west of Highway 25 on Tremaine Road/ Town Line, preserves the heritage of Ontario's farming communities.

A hexagonal barn, machinery, demonstrations and special exhibits pay homage to the farm way of life. Open late May to late September, daily 10 A.M. to 5 P.M. Admission charge, 905-878-8151.

Take a Hike: Two conservation areas offer different perspectives of the Escarpment. A high Escarpment cliff towers above Kelso Conservation Area, next to the Ontario

Agricultural Museum. Swimming, boating, fishing, hiking, picnic facilities, washrooms and downhill skiing in season at Glen Eden Ski Area. Halton Region Museum is located within the park, 905-878-5011. Admission charge.

Rattlesnake Point Conservation Area offers breathtaking views from the top of the Escarpment. Hiking trails, rock climbing (only with advance permits), picnic facilities, washrooms. To reach Rattlesnake Point, take Highway 25 south to Steeles Avenue. Continue west on Steeles for 3 kilometres to Appleby Line and then south on Appleby Line 2.5 kilometres, 905-878-1147 (weekends).

Both conservation areas are open year-round, daily 8:30 A.M. to sunset. Admission charge.

Off the Beaten Track: The Robertson screw, a socket-head screw as opposed to the traditional slot-head screw, was invented here in Milton. The Robertson Whitehouse Company, successor to the P.L. Robertson Manufacturing Company, is located on Bronte Street, northeast of Martin and Main. Look for the historic plaque and just north of it, note the Bronte Pioneer cemetery, the final resting place of Jasper and Sarah Martin, owners of the first grist mill in the area.

Fair Days: Milton's Fall Fair is held each year on the fourth weekend in September.

➤ **NORTH**

Services:

 Tim Hortons.

Pick a Peck: Fresh produce stands and pick-your-own farms abound north and south of Highway 401. Chudleigh's has turned harvesting into an event. Located 4 kilometres north on Highway 25, Chudleigh's offers apples to pick yourself, apples picked by someone else, apples pressed into cider, and apples baked into pies. Children can pet the farm animals, roll in the hay, and everyone can enjoy roasted corn-on-the-cob in season. Open July through October, daily 9 A.M. to 7 P.M.; November through June, Wednesday through Sunday 10 A.M. to 5 P.M. Some food services year-round. No admission charge, 905-878-2725.

INTERCHANGE

#324
James Snow Parkway

It 'sno(w) parkway. James Snow Parkway starts nowhere and goes nowhere. To the north it ends just above the 401 at Steeles Avenue. To the south it ends just below the 401 at Main Street. Is there a future plan that is not obvious to the casual observer?

#328
Trafalgar Road/ Halton Hills/ Georgetown/ Oakville

Trafalgar Road South leads eventually to Oakville on the shore of Lake Ontario. To the north the village of Hornby is just west of Trafalgar Road. The rural community is seriously into horses.

➤ SOUTH
Services:

A Farm of Another Kind: Van Dongen's Tree Farm, a couple of kilometres south of the 401, is open in summer daily 8 A.M. to 8 P.M. Off-season, hours are reduced, 905-821-1281.

➤ NORTH
Services:

On the Road Again: Continue east on Halton Road 8/Steeles Avenue (in this area, north of the 401) to St. Stephen's Anglican Church, just west of the Ninth Line north. Pioneers of English heritage are buried in the cemetery beside the white clapboard church. One early marker dates to 1819. Return to the 401 at IC #333, Winston Churchill Boulevard.

#333
Winston Churchill Boulevard

To the south, new subdivisions of Mississauga have grown westward to reach Winston Churchill Boulevard. To the north, the land is still cultivated.

➤ SOUTH

➤ NORTH
Services:

"Chick" It Out: Maple Lodge Farms, north on Winston Churchill Boulevard, sells fresh chicken. Open

Monday through Thursday 8:30 A.M. to 8 P.M.; Friday 8:30 A.M. to 10 P.M.; Saturday 7:30 A.M. to 5:30 P.M.; Sunday 8:30 to 5:30 P.M., 905-455-8340.

Antiques: A small antique shop, Halton Homestead, is located on Steeles Avenue just west of Winston Churchill Boulevard, 905-858-9317.

Further Afield: From 1926 to 1935, Lucy Maud Montgomery, renowned Canadian author of the popular Anne books, lived in the Presbyterian church manse at Norval to the north. In *The Selected Journals of Lucy Maud Montgomery 1921–1929*, published in 1992, Mrs. Macdonald (Montgomery married the Reverend Ewan Macdonald) chronicled life in Norval as wife, mother and author.

INTERCHANGE

#336
Mississauga Road/ Erin Mills Parkway/ Streetsville/ Mississauga

---

Mississauga Road, south of Highway 401, follows the Credit River through the village of Streetsville and terminates at Port Credit on Lake Ontario. Erin Mills Parkway, a speedy route to the Queen Elizabeth Way, branches to the right off Mississauga Road just south of the 401. Streetsville, Port Credit, and Meadowvale, north of the 401, are now part of the city of Mississauga (population 434,000).

➤ SOUTH

Services: On Mississauga Road

  Burger King · pizza pizza. · KFC

On Argentia Road to the west

 RAMADA

On Erin Mills Parkway

  HARVEY'S · swiss chalet chicken + ribs · McDonald's

  PETRO-CANADA

 Howard Johnson

Roll Back the Clock: As travellers come off the 401, they may mistakenly conclude that Mississauga Road is just new malls and business establishments. But 2.5 kilometres along, after Mississauga Road becomes Queen Street, the century-old town of Streetsville emerges.

Named after Timothy Street, Streetsville has all the charm of small-town Ontario—tree-lined streets, century homes, pioneer burying-grounds—and all the facilities of the big city—lots of restaurants, grocery stores and pharmacies.

In the graveyard of St. Andrew's Presbyterian Church at 295 Queen Street, Timothy Street is buried. Note the graveyard's huge Siamese-twin oak trees.

Picnic in the Park: Turn left off Queen Street onto any of the intersecting streets and continue east to Church Street and then south to Streetsville Memorial Park beside the Credit River. A trail follows the Credit River north to Main Street, across the bridge and north along the east side of the river.

Off the Beaten Track: Continue through Streetsville for 1.2 kilometres south of St. Andrew's Church to Barbertown Road and turn left. Follow this road 0.6 kilometres to its end at A.D.M. Milling Co. Walk out onto the bridge over the Credit River. At any time of year you'll have a first-hand look at the river, but in late October something special happens. Chinook salmon hatched upriver 4 years earlier are now on their journey back to their birthplace to spawn. Big fish (up to 30 pounds, 13.5 kg) splash and, at times, almost seem to crawl up the shallow river in their relentless quest to continue the species. Be mindful of the surrounding private property.

Special Events: On the first Saturday in June, Streetsville celebrates the founding of the town in 1820 with a Bread and Honey Festival. A thousand loaves of bread are sliced and dribbled with 40 gallons (150 litres) of honey. The festivities include a 15-kilometre "Run for the Honey" run, a parade, baking contests, craft shows and concerts, 905-858-5974.

➤ NORTH

Off the Beaten Track: Take the first right turn (Derry Road) north of the 401 and follow it for 3.5 kilometres to Meadowvale Village. Declared a Heritage Conservation District in 1980, Meadowvale retains its 19th-century appearance. No homes are open to the public, but walking-tour booklets of both Streetsville and Meadowvale, prepared by the Mississauga Heritage Foundation, are available at local tourist information centres.

Picnic in the Park: To reach the Meadowvale Conservation Park, turn left off Derry Road to Second Line West. The park is 1 kilometre north on the left beside the Credit River. Picnic tables, washrooms. No charge.

On the Road Again: Derry Road to the north and Britannia Road to the south both run east to Hurontario Street and IC #342 back to the 401.

#342
Highway 10/ Hurontario Street/ Brampton/Mississauga
★

Hurontario Street is mainstreet Mississauga. At Burnhamthorpe Road, 5.5 kilometres south, glass-and-concrete monoliths house the Mississauga Civic Centre and Square One shopping centre (350 stores, movie theatres). Queen Street, the heart of Brampton, is 9 kilometres north on Highway 10—at midday at least a 10-minute drive.

➤ SOUTH
Services:

  Sunoco

To Market: The Mississauga Central Lions Club operates a farmers' market in the parking lot of Square One from June to October, Friday 8 A.M. to 8 P.M.; Sunday 8 A.M. to 6 P.M.

➤ NORTH
Services: The first services are in the area of Derry Road.

Step Back in Time: The German Heritage Museum on Highway 10, 1.3 kilometres north of Highway 401, is housed in the 1880 Hansa House. Open only Sunday 11 A.M. to 5 P.M. Admission charge.

On the Road Again: Return to the 401 from the south by taking Highway 403 north at Eglinton Avenue or from the north by accessing Highway 410 south from Derry Road East.

#344
Highway 403/410

Highway 403 runs southwest to Oakville, Burlington and Hamilton via the Queen Elizabeth Way. Highway 410 runs north to Brampton.

Travelling eastbound on Highway 401, IC #344 exits only north to Highway 410. To reach Highway 403, go north on Highway 410 to the first exit, Courtneypark, turn around and pick up Highway 403 from southbound Highway 410. The designers evidently assumed that eastbound travellers would not wish to travel west on Highway 403.

Travelling westbound, either highway can be accessed. An entrance to the westbound 401 at IC #346/Dixie Road excludes an exit onto Highway 403 because Highway 403 exits only from the 401 express lanes, and the only Highway 401 westbound entrance from Dixie Road is via the collector lanes.

INTERCHANGE

#346
Dixie Road/Peel Road 4/ Mississauga
★

Dixie Road North skirts the western edge of Pearson International Airport and to the south runs along the eastern edge of Mississauga. Take Dixie Road north or south for food, gas and accommodation.

➤ SOUTH
Services:

Factory Outlets: Georgia Mills Factory Outlet, 5200 Dixie Road, towels, sheets, pillows, comforters. Open Monday through Friday 10 A.M. to 9 P.M.; Saturday 10 A.M. to 6 P.M.; Sunday 10 A.M. to 5 P.M., 905-629-3040. Delonghi Factory Outlet, 4500 Dixie Road, kitchen and small appliances, including Braun, Charlescraft, Regal. Open Monday, Tuesday 10 A.M. to 5 P.M.; Wednesday through Friday 10 A.M. to 8 P.M.; Saturday 10 A.M. to 5 P.M.; Sunday noon to 5 P.M., 905-238-8944.

➤ NORTH
Services:

 Sunoco

On the Road Again: The entrance to the 401 from Dixie Road is via the collector lanes. From these collector lanes, there is no exit to Highways 403 and 410. See IC #344.

For a list of Metropolitan Toronto interchanges, see page 158.

#365
Allen Road/Toronto

Allen Road has a long history. It was once meant to be a western parkway to downtown Toronto. But priorities change and what was once called the Spadina Expressway and then the Allen Expressway now ends at Eglinton Avenue. Allen Road runs just to the east of Yorkdale Shopping Centre, Toronto's first indoor shopping centre. The 250 stores and services in the mall include department stores, independent retailers, restaurants, banks, a gas station and movie theatres. The hours for the mall are Monday to Friday 10 A.M. to 9 P.M.; Saturday 9:30 A.M. to 6 P.M.; Sunday noon to 5 P.M.

The shopping centre is directly south of the 401 on Yorkdale Road. To reach it from the west take Dufferin Street south, IC #364. To reach it from the east take Allen Road south.

Collector Lanes Versus Express Lanes

Across the north of Toronto, the many lanes of Highway 401 are divided into two routes, the collector lanes and the express lanes. There are many transfer points between the two, and motorists may choose to travel in either set of lanes. All signs in the core or express lanes are green; those in the collector lanes are blue.

Airport Information

To check on arriving and departing flights from Pearson International Airport, tune into CFYZ 1280 AM on your radio dial. Reports are bilingual.

#373
Leslie Street/Toronto

As the city of Toronto developed and expanded in all directions, city planners retained acres of natural parkland along the valleys of the city's once great but now diminished rivers. Leslie Street cuts through the valleys created by the rivers and creeks of the Don River system.

➤ SOUTH

Services:

 The Prince Hotel on York Mills Road

Heritage Home: The Tudor-style Locke House immediately south on Leslie Street barely survived the construction of the 401. Expropriated in 1964 for the freeway, it suffered from neglect and vandalism for many years until the Federation of

Ontario Naturalists restored it in the late 1970s. The house sits on land that was originally part of Ontario Premier George Henry's Oriole Farm; he built it as a wedding gift for his daughter in 1933. The second building on the site, Goodwin House, believed to be the oldest remaining house in North York, was rescued and moved by the Federation in 1982 from its original site on Yonge Street south of York Mills. The Federation operates its headquarters from the two buildings. A small gift shop in Locke House sells naturalist publications, cassettes and educational materials, and the knowledgeable staff is always willing to answer questions. Open Monday through Friday 9 A.M. to 5 P.M., 416-444-8419. Turn left at the first stoplight (Lesmill Road) and make another quick left into the driveway.

Take a Hike: In Edward's Garden, at Leslie Street and Lawrence Avenue, 3.5 kilometres south, volunteers give guided tours of the gardens, May through September, Tuesday and Thursday at 11 A.M. and 2 P.M. Walking trails extend from Wilket Creek south to the wide-open spaces of Sunnybrook Park and Serena Gundy Park. No charges for the park or tours. Enter from Leslie Street, just south of Lawrence. Gift shop. Seasonal restaurant, 416-397-1340.

➤ **NORTH**

Services: West on Sheppard Avenue

Hospital: North York General Hospital, 4001 Leslie Street, 416-756-6000.

INTERCHANGE

#389
Meadowvale Road/ Scarborough

Meadowvale Road is on the eastern edge of Scarborough.

➤ **SOUTH**

➤ **NORTH**

Services:

Go Wild: The Metro Toronto Zoo is located 2.5 kilometres north. More than 5,000 animals representing 559 species live in the 690-acre (280 ha) site. That's a lot of ground to cover, so don't plan on a quick visit if you want to see the whole zoo. Open every day except Christmas. Summer hours, daily 9 A.M. to 7 P.M. Winter hours are shorter. Admission charge, 416-392-5900.

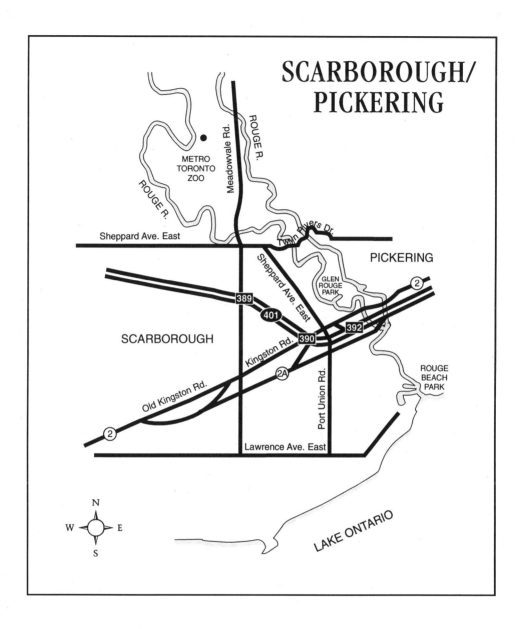

SCARBOROUGH/ PICKERING

On the Road Again: Instead of returning to the 401, turn east on Sheppard Avenue and follow Twyn Rivers Road along a steep and winding route over two narrow bridges, down into the valley and back up to Whites Road, and return to the 401 at IC #394. In spring, summer and early fall, wildflowers are abundant. In fall, the valley is a blaze of colour. Parking lots and hiking trails.

Toronto Radio Stations

AM

590	CJCL	Sports
640	AM640	Top 40/Talk
680	CFTR	News/Traffic Report
740	CBL	Multiformat (CBC)
860	CJBC	French Language
1010	CFRB	Talk (Stereo)
1050	CHUM	Oldies (Stereo)
1540	CHIN	Multicultural

FM

88.9	CIRV	Multicultural/Multilingual
91.1	CJRT	Educational/Classic/Folk/ Blues/Jazz
92.5	CISS	New Country
97.3	CJEZ	Easy Listening/Classic Hits
98.1	CHFI	Contemporary
99.9	CKFM	Contemporary
100.7	CHIN	Multicultural/Multilingual
102.1	CFNY	Alternative Album Rock
104.5	CHUM	Album-oriented Rock
107.1	Q107	Album-oriented Rock

INTERCHANGE

#390
Highway 2/
Port Union Road

Interchange #390 exits from the eastbound 401; IC #392 exits from the westbound 401. They both end up in the same place and each one accesses Highway 2 and 2A, Port Union Road, Sheppard Avenue and Kingston Road (Highway 2). From here, Highway 2 to the east runs parallel to and north of the 401 and to the west dips south of the 401 and continues southwest toward downtown Toronto as Kingston Road. Sheppard Avenue begins north of the 401 where Port Union Road stops, and then bends west to run parallel to the 401 across the top of Toronto.

➤ **SOUTH** on Port Union Road
Services:

Picnic in the Park: Follow Port Union Road south to Lawrence Avenue East. Turn left and follow the signs to Rouge Beach Park (4 kilometres). Here the meandering Rouge River finally reaches Lake Ontario. Picnic facilities, supervised beach, washrooms, fishing and great bird-watching. No charge.

➤ **EAST** on Highway 2
Services:

Take a Hike: East 1 kilometre along Highway 2, you can reach the Rouge Valley through Glen Rouge Park. This park is mainly a camping facility, but you can park here and follow the hiking trails along the Rouge River toward Twyn Rivers Drive and even as far north as the Metro Toronto Zoo. See IC #389.

On the Road Again: Return to the 401 from Highway 2/Kingston Road East at Whites Road, IC #394. South of the 401 there is no route across the Rouge Valley.

INTERCHANGE

#392
Sheppard Avenue/
Highway 2/2A

For eastbound travellers, IC #390 is identified as the exit for Highway 2 and Port Union Road. For westbound travellers, IC #392 is the exit for Highway 2 and Sheppard Avenue. See IC #390 for the relationship between these exits and streets and for service information.

Sheppard Avenue swings west and crosses Meadowvale Road. Take Meadowvale Road north to the Metro Toronto Zoo (see IC #389).

INTERCHANGE

#394
Whites Road/
Pickering

Whites Road is the most westerly exit to Pickering and should be used by eastbound travellers to reach the Pickering Town Centre.

➤ SOUTH
Services:

Picnic in the Park: Frenchman's Bay is accessible from Petticoat Creek Conservation Area at the foot of White's Road (1.2 kilometres). Swimming, picnic facilities, walking trails and washrooms. Seasonal. Admission charge.

➤ NORTH
Services:

 just west on Highway 2

On the Road Again: In the not-so-distant past, Highway 2 was just a country road. Today industry and commerce are more familiar than farmland on this route from Toronto to Oshawa.

INTERCHANGE

#397
Liverpool Road/
Durham Road 29/
Pickering
★

Liverpool Road leads into Pickering and the Pickering Town Centre, but only from the 401 west. With no exit to Liverpool Road from the 401 east, eastbound travellers should exit at IC #394 for access to the Pickering Town Centre.

➤ SOUTH
Services:

Picnic in the Park: At the foot of Liverpool Road, sea gulls and Canada geese share the lakefront park. Picnic tables. Washrooms. No charge.

➤ NORTH
Services:

  Burger King

  (Esso)

All services at Pickering Town Centre (280-plus stores) or on Highway 2.

On the Road Again: On Highway 2 east to Brock Road, roadside stands sell fresh fruits and vegetables in season.

#399
Brock Road/
Durham Road 1/
Pickering

Brock Road is Pickering's most easterly exit.

➤ SOUTH
Services:

Play Awhile: Turn right on Bayly Street from Brock Road South for the Pickering Playing Fields, an activity centre with mini-putt and batting cages. Seasonal from April to October. Hours vary. Admission charge, 905-420-9090.

Take a Tour: At the Pickering Nuclear Station, 3.5 kilometres south on Brock Road, interactive videos, a full-scale model of a Candu reactor, displays, computer games, films, and bus tours (call ahead to check availability) introduce visitors of all ages to nuclear power. Picnic tables. No charge. Open Monday through Friday 9 A.M. to 4 P.M., 905-839-0465.

Picnic in the Park: Turn left after leaving the Pickering Nuclear Station and continue to Sandy Beach Road and the Alex Robertson Community Park. Picnic facilities. No charge.

➤ NORTH
Services:

Bargain Hunt: There is no admission charge at the Pickering Flea Market and Antique Fair (730 vendors at the market, 100 dealers at the fair) in the Metro East Trade Centre on the east side of Brock Road just north of the 401. Sunday only, 9 A.M. to 5 P.M., 905-427-0754.

On the Road Again: On Highway 2 east, watch for Elizabeth Street and Pickering Village, a street of small businesses housed in historic buildings. Note the early brickwork. Godiva Antiques & Gifts, located in an 1843 stone house at 22 Linton Avenue, tempts collectors of Canadiana. Open Tuesday through Saturday 10 A.M. to 5 P.M.; Sunday 1 P.M. to 5 P.M., 905-683-1018.

INTERCHANGE

#401
Westney Road/Ajax

This is it! Exit 401 on the 401. South on Westney Road a commercial and industrial area gives way to lakeview residences. To the north, beyond Highway 2, farmers compete with land developers for space.

➤ SOUTH
Services:

Factory Outlets: *McLeans Wholesale Outlet*, 384 Westney Road. Party supplies, toys, games, novelties, small kitchen accessories, T-shirts, sweatshirts and moccasins. Open Monday through Saturday 8 A.M. to 4:30 P.M., 905-427-2388. *Sure-Fit Factory Outlet*, 458 Fairall Street (one block south of the 401, left off Westney Road). Bedspreads, duvet covers, draperies, bolts and remnants of fabric. Open Tuesday through Saturday 10 A.M. to 4:30 P.M., 905-683-1501.

Say Cheese: Thursday is best at Reid's Milky Way Dairy Products on the northwest corner of Fairall Street and Westney Road. This branch store of a Belleville dairy is stocked with cheese, milk, ice cream, and juices. Fresh curd is delivered on Thursday and sells out before the week is over. Open Monday through Friday 9 A.M. to 8 P.M.; Saturday 9 A.M. to 6 P.M., 905-428-2468.

➤ NORTH
Services:

On the Road Again: Westney Road South curves east and meets

Harwood Avenue, north of Ajax Waterfront Park (see IC #403). Fresh-picked fruit and vegetables—strawberries in early summer, corn and tomatoes and beans midsummer, and then apples in the fall—are available at roadside stands on Highway 2 east heading toward Ajax.

#403
Harwood Avenue/Ajax

Ajax was named after the British warship, *H.M.S. Ajax*, and developed around a Second World War munitions factory. To the south, acres of parkland line Lake Ontario, and to the north beyond Highway 2, the town abuts rural Ontario.

➤ SOUTH
Services:

Harwood Place Mall

Hospital: Ajax & Pickering General Hospital, Harwood Avenue South, 905-683-2320.
Picnic in the Park: At Ajax Waterfront Park, you can watch sailboats on the lake, walk 3 kilometres of waterfront trails, or swim in Lake Ontario's frigid waters. The park is straight south 3.5 kilometres

on Harwood Avenue. Parking areas both east and west on Lake Driveway. Washrooms.

➤ NORTH
Services:

Radio Station: CHOO AM 1390
Roll Back the Clock: Many of the small houses on the streets immediately north of the 401 and east and west off Harwood Avenue remain essentially unchanged from the years 1942 and 1943 when they were constructed as housing for the workers at DIL (Defence Industries Limited). Workers who lived in these modest homes filled millions of shells for Second World War battles.
On the Road Again: At Picov Downs, 2 kilometres east on Highway 2 at 380 Kingston Road, quarter horses race each Sunday at 1:30 P.M. from mid-May to mid-October. Admission charge, 905-686-0948. Visit Picov's Greenhouse next door. Roadside stands featuring fresh fruit and vegetables are plentiful, east on Highway 2.

#410
Highway 12/Brock
Street/Whitby

You are halfway there! On the 820 kilometres of Highway 401 from the

Ontario/Michigan border to the Ontario/Quebec border, IC #410 is the midpoint.

Highway 401 bisects Whitby. The older business section is north of the 401. The port and the former railway station are south.

➤ SOUTH

Services: In GO Station

OPP: At 1301 Henry Street (access past the GO Station parking), 905-668-3388.

Hospital: Whitby General Hospital, 300 Gordon Street. Emergency services 8 A.M. to 10 P.M. only, 905-668-6831.

Newspaper: *Whitby Free Press*, weekly on Wednesday.

Picnic in the Park: Follow Brock Street south for 2 kilometres, past Victoria Street (the first set of lights) and the flocks of Canada geese puddling in the shallows of the harbour, to a small park with picnic tables, playground equipment, outdoor washrooms and a telephone.

Take a Hike: Go west 3 kilometres from the intersection of Brock and Victoria Streets to a popular bird-watching spot, Lynde Shores Conservation Area. Walk the boardwalk into Lynde Creek or spy on spring migrants from the viewing platforms on the edge of Cranberry Marsh. Hiking, fishing, canoeing, skating, picnic tables, barbecues, washrooms. No charge.

For Art's Sake: The Station Gallery is located in the old Whitby train station at the northeast corner of Victoria and Henry Streets. Open Tuesday through Friday 12 noon to 5 P.M.; Tuesday through Thursday 6 P.M. to 9 P.M.; Saturday and Sunday 2 P.M. to 5 P.M., 905-668-4185.

➤ NORTH

Services:

Many services on Highway 2 (Dundas Street), east or west.

North on Brock Street and west on Mary Street, a number of turn-of-the-century homes moved here, refurbished and connected, form a unique commercial block of trendy shops, boutiques and restaurants. The complex is known as Pearson Lanes.

Tourist Information: A year-round tourist centre is located at 900 Brock Street (just north of the 401). Ask for "A Guide To Our Historical & Architectural Heritage." Open Monday to Friday 9:30 A.M. to 5:30 P.M.; Saturday 10 A.M. to 6 P.M. Summer hours, Victoria Day to Labour Day, Monday to Friday 9 A.M. to 8 P.M.; Saturday, Sunday and holidays 10 A.M. to 6 P.M. Picnic tables. Washrooms. 905-668-0552.

On the Road Again: Highway 2 continues east parallel to the 401.

#412
Thickson Road/
Durham Road 26/
Whitby

Thickson Road acts as a dividing line between Oshawa to the east and Whitby to the west, but it is hard to tell where one stops and the next begins.

➤ SOUTH
Services: On Bloor Street West (east from Thickson Road)

Off the Beaten Track: Sir William Stephenson, "The Man Called Intrepid" and director of British Security Co-ordination from 1941 to 1946, is remembered in Intrepid Park in Whitby. On the site of Camp X, commemorative plaques acknowledge the training schools for Allied spies that operated here during the Second World War. Take Thickson Road south to Wentworth Street and turn left. Follow Wentworth Street to Boundary Road. Turn right and follow Boundary Road past the large LCBO warehouse. The park and memorial are just beyond. See also IC #416 for the Robert Stuart Aeronautical Museum.

➤ NORTH
Services:

 Sunoco

Whitby Mall

On Champlain Avenue just north of the 401 east of Thickson Road.

On the Road Again: The Oshawa Centre (170-plus stores) is on Highway 2 east at Stevenson Road.

#416
Park Road/Oshawa

Oshawa has not been a one-horse town since R.S. McLaughlin began manufacturing horseless carriages in 1907 at the McLaughlin Carriage Company. In 1918, McLaughlin's successful automotive venture became part of General Motors, with R.S. at the helm of the Canadian operation. Oshawa, "The City That Moto-vates," was on its way to becoming a one-industry town.

➤ SOUTH
Services:

From Park Road westbound travellers may access the motels on Bloor Street West or Champlain Avenue listed in IC #412.

➤ NORTH

Services:

Radio Stations: CKDO AM 1350, CKGE FM 94.9

Off the Beaten Track: The Oshawa Aeronautical, Military and Industrial Museum is located at the Oshawa airport on the site of a Second World War training facility for Allied flyers. The collection includes period uniforms and equipment, and displays reflecting the role of industry, particularly that of General Motors, in the war effort. Open Easter through November 30, Tuesday through Saturday, noon to 5 P.M.; Sunday 1 P.M. to 5 P.M. 1000 Stevenson Road, 905-728-6199. Admission charge. Next door, artefacts in a private museum, the Robert Stuart Aeronautical Museum, include Camp X memorabilia (see IC #412). Open Saturday and Sunday 9 A.M. to 8 P.M. Take Park Road north to Rossland Road. Turn left on Rossland, and then right on Stevenson Road.

On the Road Again: The interchanges in Oshawa are very close together. Return to the 401 at any of the next three main streets.

INTERCHANGE

#417
Simcoe Street/Oshawa

Simcoe Street is Oshawa's main north-south artery, running south from beyond the former McLaughlin residence, Parkwoods, past the downtown core at King and Simcoe, to Benjamin Wilson's 1790 settlement on the lakefront. The exits to Oshawa are sometimes confusing. Pay attention to the signs as you exit. To reach Simcoe Street from the westbound 401, exit at IC #418, Ritson Road.

➤ SOUTH

Services:

Picnic in the Park: At the foot of Simcoe Street (about 5 kilometres from the 401) on the Lake Ontario shore, Lakeview Park has something for everyone. A children's playground, supervised beach with change rooms, picnic tables, benches and a waterfront walking path. No charge.

Step Back in Time: Adjacent to Lakeview Park, Henry House, Robinson House and Guy House, collectively known as the Oshawa Sydenham Museum, preserve Oshawa's history. Thomas Henry, his wife and their 12 children lived in the stone cottage here for many years. Open mid-May to mid-October, daily 1 P.M. to 5 P.M. Rest of the year, Sunday through Friday,

OSHAWA

PARKWOOD

Rossland Rd.

Bond St.

King St.

King St.

Stevenson Rd.

Park Rd. S.

Simcoe St.

Ritson Rd.

CANADIAN AUTOMOTIVE MUSEUM

Harmony Rd.

412

416 417 418

419

Thickson Rd.

Bloor St. W.

Stevenson

Simcoe St. S.

Bloor St. E.

401

MCLAUGHLIN BAY WILDLIFE RESERVE

LAKE ONTARIO

LAKEVIEW PARK

OSHAWA SYDENHAM MUSEUM

1 P.M. to 5 P.M. Admission charge, 905-436-7624.

➤ NORTH
Services:

  pizza pizza.

 KFC   Tim Hortons.

Hospital: Oshawa General Hospital, 24 Alma Street (off Simcoe North), 905-576-8711.

Tourist Information: The Oshawa Chamber of Commerce operates a year-round tourist information centre at 50 Richmond Street East (two blocks north of King Street, east of Simcoe). Open Monday through Friday 9 A.M. to 5 P.M., 905-728-1683. Ask for the brochure "Reminiscences of Early Downtown Oshawa, An Historical Walking Tour."

For Art's Sake: The Robert McLaughlin Gallery in the Civic Centre on Bagot Street houses a collection of Canadian art that specializes in the art of the Painters Eleven, Ontario's first group of abstract artists. Open Tuesday, Wednesday, Friday 10 A.M. to 5 P.M.; Thursday 10 A.M. to 9 P.M.; Saturday and Sunday noon to 4 P.M. No charge, 905-576-3000.

Step Back in Time: In the Canadian Automotive Museum at 99 Simcoe Street North, a 1914 Galt Gas Electric rubs fenders with a 1969 Daimler limousine. Open April through September, Monday through Friday 9 A.M. to 5 P.M.; Saturday and Sunday 10 A.M. to 6 P.M.; October through March, closed on Mondays. Admission charge, 905-576-1222.

Parkwood, R.S. McLaughlin's estate at 270 Simcoe Street North, shows just what money could buy. The stately 55-room mansion, set on 12 beautifully landscaped acres (5 ha), preserves a record of gracious, early 20th-century living. Open June through August, Tuesday through Sunday 10:30 A.M. to 4 P.M.; September through May, Tuesday through Friday, and Sunday 1:30 P.M.

to 4 P.M. Admission charge. Tea and lunch are served in either the Garden Tea House or the Greenhouse Tea Room, depending on the season, 905-579-1311.

INTERCHANGE

#418 Ritson Road/ Oshawa

When Edward Skae opened his general store at the crossroads of the military route from Kingston to Toronto and the original Mississauga trail to Lake Scugog (now King and Simcoe), the area was known as Skae's Corners. Historians claim that when the settlement applied for a post office in 1842, the word Oshawa, meaning "the crossing between waters," was chosen as the official name. Westbound travellers should exit at Ritson Road for Simcoe Street.

➤ **SOUTH**

➤ **NORTH**
Services:

   Sunoco

On the Road Again: To the east, Bloor Street leads to the Harmony Road/Bloor Street East entrance to the 401, IC #419.

INTERCHANGE

#419
Bloor Street/
Harmony Road/Oshawa

Harmony Road/Bloor Street is the most easterly exit to Oshawa and a bit confusing to the uninitiated. Sometimes Bloor Street is north of the 401; sometimes it is south of the 401. Pay attention to the signs.

➤ SOUTH

Take a Hike: From the early days of Colonel Sam's (R.S. McLaughlin's) automotive successes, General Motors has dominated Oshawa life. In return, GM has proven itself a good corporate citizen. Beside the company's new glass-and-steel corporate headquarters on the lake side of the 401, east of IC #419, the 100-acre (40 ha) McLaughlin Bay Wildlife Reserve is taking shape as a joint effort between GM and area environmentalists. To reach the reserve, go west on Bloor Street, turn left on Farewell Street, continue south to Colonel Sam Drive and turn left. The total distance is 3.5 kilometres. Park in the visitors' lot.

Nature trails, walkways and viewing platforms.

➤ NORTH
Services: on Bloor Street East

On the Road Again: There is no route south around McLaughlin Bay to the next eastern interchange. Highway 2 north of the 401 leads east to Courtice Road, IC #425.

INTERCHANGE

#425
Courtice Road/Durham
Road 34/Courtice

Courtice, to the north, once a small village, is now part of the much larger Municipality of Clarington, which includes the urban centres of Bowmanville, Newcastle and Orono, as well as the rural areas from the eastern border of Oshawa to east of Newcastle.

➤ SOUTH
Services:

Picnic in the Park: Darlington Park Road leads only to Darlington Provincial Park, a Lake Ontario park with both overnight campsites and day-use areas. The park offers swimming, boating (including boat rental), fishing, picnic facilities, washrooms, an information centre in an original log cabin, and a pioneer cemetery. Admission charge, 905-436-2036.

Take a Tour: Although the Darlington Generating Station is located at the foot of Holt Road (IC #428), take Courtice Road south, the South Service Road east and Park Road south to reach the information centre. Visitors are welcome year-round, Monday through Friday 9 A.M. to 4 P.M. Call ahead to determine the availability of bus tours. No charge, 1-800-461-0034.

➢ NORTH

Bargain Hunt: Courtice Flea Market is open year-round, Saturday 9:30 A.M. to 4 P.M.; Sunday 9:30 A.M. to 5 P.M. Turn left at Bloor Street, 2 kilometres north on Courtice Road.

On the Road Again: Follow Highway 2 east and return to the 401 by one of the Bowmanville exits, IC #431 or IC #432.

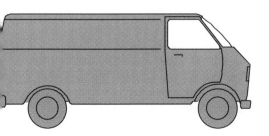

INTERCHANGE

#428
Holt Road

Holt Road does not exist north of the 401. To the south it leads only to the guard house of the Darlington Generating Station. Visitors are welcome at the CANDU generating station information centre but should access it from the service road. See IC #425 for directions, 1-800-461-0034.

On the Road Again: To return to the 401 east, continue east on the service road to IC #431.

INTERCHANGE

#431
Waverley Road/
Bowmanville

Waverley Road is the first of two exits to downtown Bowmanville. To the south, Waverley Road ends at St. Mary's Cement.

➢ SOUTH
Services:

Fifth Wheel Truck Stop, open 24 hours.

➤ NORTH
Services:

Other services in Bowmanville, 3 kilometres

Take a Hike: North of the 401, take the left fork of the road, Regional Road 57, north to King Street. Turn right on King Street and right again after 0.6 kilometres at Roenigk Drive. The Bowmanville Valley Conservation Area is to the left beside Bowmanville Creek. Picnic facilities, hiking trails, washrooms. No charge.

Step Back in Time: At the Bowmanville Museum, a particularly fine piano manufactured by an early Bowmanville company, the Dominion Organ and Piano Company, is on exhibit, along with an extensive doll collection that includes skating dolls, kewpie dolls and even Dionne quintuplet dolls—more than 2,000 in all. The museum is located in a house built in 1860 at 37 Silver Street. Open Tuesday to Sunday and holiday Mondays, 11 A.M. to 4 P.M. Admission charge, 905-623-2734.

Roll Back the Clock: Octagonal buildings were the latest thing in mid-19th-century Ontario. In his book, *A Home for all: or, the Gravel Wall, and Octagon Mode of Building*, American Orson Fowler touted the eight-sided structures as a cure-all for ill health and nasty dispositions.

A large stuccoed house just north of King Street on the west side of Division Street, built as an octagonal parsonage in 1864, remains relatively unchanged today. The barn at the Ontario Agricultural Museum in Milton (IC #320) and the house at 45 Parliament in East Colborne (IC #497) are further examples of the fad.

INTERCHANGE

#432
Liberty Street/
Bowmanville/
Port Darlington

Liberty Street exits to downtown Bowmanville.

➤ SOUTH
Services: In Port Darlington

Picnic in the Park: Bowmanville Harbour Conservation Area, on the edge of Lake Ontario in Port Darlington, has picnic tables, a boat launch, washrooms, and lots of resident Canada geese. A Grade 12 carpentry class from Courtice Secondary School built the viewing platform across from the boat launch. Take

Lake Road east off Liberty Street directly south of the 401 and turn right on Port Darlington Road. No charge.

➤ NORTH

Services:

  serving

On Highway 2 east

Hospital: Memorial Hospital, 47 Liberty Street, 905-623-3331.

Tourist Information: Information is available at the tourist and general information centre on Liberty Street just north of the 401. Open year-round, Labour Day through May, Monday through Friday regular office hours; June to Labour Day, extended weekday hours and Saturday and Sunday, 905-623-0733.

Go Wild: The Bowmanville Zoo, established in 1919, is Canada's oldest operating zoo. It all began as a promotion to encourage children to eat Cream of Barley cereal. John Morden, president of John McKay Ltd., the mill producing the cereal, opened a tourist camp on a nearby farm to attract families with children, his marketing target.

Swings and slides to amuse the children led to the acquisition of a few animals for them to pet, and then a few more. Before following the signs to the zoo north of the 401, turn right on Baseline Road and left at Simpson Avenue. The Cream of Barley Mill is still beside Soper Creek, and is now home to the Visual Arts Centre of Clarington. Retrace your steps to Liberty Street to follow the signs to the zoo. Open May through September daily and weekends in October, 10 A.M. to 4, 5, or 6 P.M. depending on the season. During the summer months, the lions are fed at 5 P.M., 905-623-5655.

On the Road Again: For a rural "fix," take Highway 2 east as it continues north of the 401 to Port Hope intersecting each artery to the 401 along the way.

INTERCHANGE

#435
Bennett Road

Bennett Road leads south to the planned private community of Wilmot Creek. To the north, Bennett Road meets Highway 2.

➤ SOUTH

➤ NORTH

INTERCHANGE

#436
Highways 35/115/ Orono/Lindsay/ Peterborough

Highways 35 and 115 are combined into one four-lane divided highway leading only north. Access is not limited to interchanges, but turnarounds are possible only at interchanges. Lindsay and Peterborough are beyond our reach.

➤ NORTH

Services: At the first exit, Highway 2 leads to Bowmanville (west) and Newcastle (east). At the second exit, a turnaround is possible.

The above services are available beyond the second exit but you must travel north to the next interchange to return south.

The Village Bake Shop and Tea Room on Main Street in Orono is open Tuesday through Thursday 8 A.M. to 6 P.M.; Friday 8 A.M. to 9 P.M. and Saturday 8 A.M. to 5 P.M., 905-983-9779.

Go Wild: At Jungle Cat World, lions, Siberian tigers, leopards and panthers rule. Free-roaming deer, goats, donkeys and sheep accept handouts and hugs. Playground, daily feeding schedules and presentations. Take the Clarke Road exit (Concession 6), 11 kilometres north. Open March to October, daily 10 A.M. to 6 P.M., 905-983-5016.

Take a Hike: Each year, six million seedlings, mostly pine and spruce, grown at the Orono Forest Station leave home to reforest Crown lands, municipal and conservation authority forests and even some private lands (conditions apply). Visitors are welcome at the station for tours of the nursery. Take the Main Street exit off Highway 35/115 (8.2 kilometres) and turn left at Princess Street. Open Monday through Friday 8 A.M. to 4:30 P.M., 905-983-9147. Pick up a brochure at the office for the station's Linton Trail, a 5-kilometre walking trail entered from the 5th Concession Road. Follow the dirt road south from the office entrance, and cross the concession road. No charge.

Fair Days: On the weekend after Labour Day, Orono continues an agricultural fall fair tradition begun in 1852.

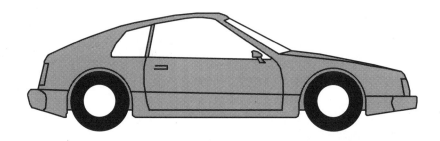

INTERCHANGE

#440
Mill Street/
Durham Road 17/
Newcastle/
Bond Head

Directly north of the 401 in the village of Newcastle, fine 19th-century homes contrast with the surrounding housing developments. To the south, in the original harbour community of Bond Head, the Port of Newcastle Marina on the west side of the creek caters to the boating crowd.

➤ SOUTH

Picnic in the Park: At the foot of Mill Street in Bond Head (on the east side of the creek), walk the pier, or picnic on the small beach. No swimming allowed.

➤ NORTH
Services:

Roll Back the Clock: From the gracious cobblestone home at 285 Mill Street, Daniel Massey founded a dynasty whose members would leave their mark in industry, politics

and the theatre. The Newcastle Foundry and Machine Manufactory operated in the large redbrick building on the south side of King Street at Beaver Street before its move to Toronto in 1879–80. The company was known in later years as Massey-Ferguson, a large and, for many years, successful agricultural implement manufacturer. The Right Honourable Vincent Massey, Canada's first native-born governor-general, and Raymond Massey, the actor, were members of this family. **On the Road Again:** Highway 2 runs parallel to and north of the 401 to Newtonville, IC #448, Welcome, IC #461 and Port Hope, IC #464.

INTERCHANGE

#448
Newtonville Road/
Newtonville

Newtonville Road leads to Newton-ville, a village (population 475) 1 kilometre north of the 401.

➤ SOUTH

➤ NORTH
Services:

INTERCHANGE

#456
Wesleyville Road

Exit here and you'll find more rural Ontario. One kilometre north, Highway 2 leads east to Port Hope and west to Newcastle and Bowmanville.

➤ SOUTH

➤ NORTH

INTERCHANGE

#461
Highway 2/
Port Hope/
Welcome

It's a toss-up which is the greater attraction in Port Hope, the town's well-preserved 19th-century buildings or its impressive river, the Ganaraska. Since the river runs right through the downtown area, travellers can enjoy both at the same time. Port Hope is about 3 kilometres south on Highway 2.

➤ SOUTH

Services:

Tourist Information: The Port Hope and District Chamber of Commerce operates a tourist information centre at 35 John Street. Open year-round, Monday through Friday 9 A.M. to 5 P.M.; July and August, Saturday 9 A.M. to 5 P.M.; Sunday 10 A.M. to 5 P.M., 905-885-5519.

Roll Back the Clock: Port Hope was once Toronto! And it was also Ganaraske and Cochingomink and Smith's Creek and finally, in 1819, years after the arrival of the first United Empire Loyalists, the name was changed to Port Hope to honour Colonel Henry Hope. Many buildings on Walton Street, the main business street, date to the 1850s. Walking-tour booklets are sold at the tourist information office.

Antiques: Port Hope boasts about a dozen antique shops on Walton Street and the neighbouring side streets. Ask the first shop you visit for the brochure "Antiques & Decorative Arts in Port Hope."

➤ NORTH

Services:

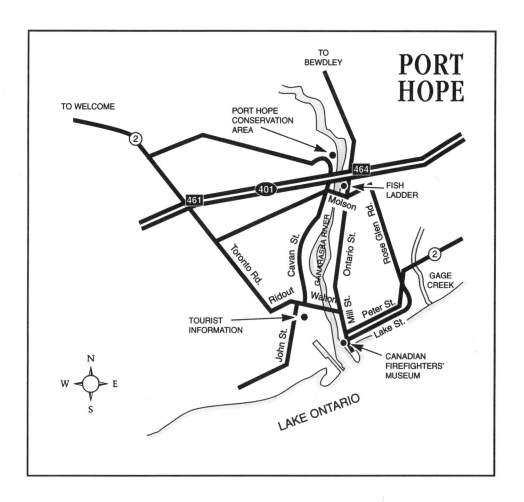

PORT HOPE

TO BEWDLEY

TO WELCOME

②

PORT HOPE CONSERVATION AREA

464

401

461

FISH LADDER

Molson

Ganaraska River

Rose Glen Rd.

Toronto Rd.

Cavan St.

Ontario St.

②

GAGE CREEK

Ridout

Walton

Mill St.

Peter St.

Lake St.

TOURIST INFORMATION

John St.

CANADIAN FIREFIGHTERS' MUSEUM

N
W E
S

LAKE ONTARIO

On the Road Again: Walton Street intersects Mill Street, which runs north to the 401 (IC #464).

"A small stream, which here falls into the Lake, has formed a valley, in which the town is located. The harbour formed at the mouth of this stream is shallow, but safe and commodious. Port Hope is a very pretty town; on the western side, the hills rise gradually one above another. The highest summit, which is called 'Fort Orion,' affords a fine prospect, and overlooks the country for a great distance around."
—*Hunter's Panoramic Guide from Niagara to Quebec*, W.S. Hunter, 1857

#464
Highway 28/Port Hope/Peterborough

Highway 28 meets Highway 115 and continues north to Peterborough. To the south, Ontario and Mill Streets lead to downtown Port Hope.

The shallow and safe harbour at the mouth of the Ganaraska River, through which agricultural products, lumber and whisky passed, played a large role in the 19th-century prosperity of Port Hope. The resulting fortunes built a grand town.

➤ SOUTH

Services:

Most services in Port Hope.

Hospital: Port Hope & District Hospital, 53 Wellington Street, 905-885-6371.

To Market: In July and August on Saturday mornings, local produce is sold at a farmers' market in the parking lot behind the Town Hall.

Step Back in Time: The Canadian Firefighters Museum at 95 Mill Street (east side of the river, south of Peter Street) traces the history of firefighting in Canada from 1830 to 1955.

Open June to Labour Day, daily 10 A.M. to 4 P.M. No charge.

Picnic in the Park: There are two public beach areas. East Beach at the foot of Madison has a sandy beach, picnic tables and a playground area. For West Beach, continue south from John Street.

Take a Hike: From Peter Street (Highway 2 east of Mill Street) turn south on Hope Street to Lake Street. A walking trail high above the Lake Ontario shore leads to another parking area at Rose Glen Road and the wetland around Gages Creek. No charge.

Fair Days: Port Hope holds a fall fair at the Agricultural Park the second weekend in September.

Special Event: Each year on the second Saturday in April, regardless of the weather, canoes and kayaks compete against homemade crafts in a crazy river race, the "Float Your Fanny Down the Ganny." View the race from anywhere along the river—try the park south on Cavan Street. The race begins at 10 A.M. and ends around 3 P.M.

Season's Best: In late March and early April, thousands of spawning rainbow trout travel up the Ministry of Natural Resources Fish Ladder at Corbett's Dam just south of the 401. Take Molson Street (the first street south of and parallel to the 401) west of Highway 28 and turn right at Cavan Street. A small parking lot and viewing area are to the right. No charge. The mill across the river was built around 1855 by Thomas Molson (of the Montreal brewing Molsons) as a distillery to produce Port Hope whisky. The whisky made with the waters of the Ganaraska enjoyed great popularity in 19th-century Europe.

Take Another Hike: Just north of Corbett's Dam and north of the 401—although best accessed from Cavan Street—the Port Hope Conservation Area offers hiking trails and picnic places. Pick up the most southerly section of the Ganaraska Hiking Trail here and follow the Ganaraska River to downtown Port Hope.

➤ **NORTH**
Services:

On the Road Again: Highway 2 east leads to Cobourg, passing by the Northumberland Mall (70-plus stores).

INTERCHANGE

#472
Burnham Street/ Northumberland Road 18/ Cobourg/Gores Landing

---

County Road 18 leads north to Gores Landing and the popular cottage resort area of Rice Lake. Burnham Street leads south to Highway 2 and downtown Cobourg (population 15,000). Also, see IC #474 for Cobourg.

Great Blue Heron

The great blue heron is Canada's largest heron. The lean, slate-grey birds can sometimes be seen standing motionless at the shallow edges of marshes and ponds of Southern Ontario. For the beginning bird-watcher, herons are easy to identify. They are big: they stand at least 4 feet (120 cm) tall and have a wingspan of 6 feet (180 cm). They are not flighty; you may find them either standing tall and still or wading cautiously as they fish in the shallows. They are handsome—more grey than blue, with a black stripe extending from the base of the bill over the eye and ending in two long, slender black feathers trailing from the back of the head. Their flight silhouette is easily recognizable; they fold their great long necks back on their shoulders and let their legs trail out behind.

There is an easy way to remember the relative geographic positions of the towns of Cobourg and Colbourne. The 401 exits are numbered west to east; thus Cobourg, whose "b" comes alphabetically before Colbourne's "l," will be reached first, from west to east.

➤ SOUTH

Services: On Highway 2 east

On Highway 2 west

 Burger King

Northumberland Mall (70-plus stores)

Newspapers: *Cobourg Daily Star*, Monday through Friday. *Northumberland News*, Wednesday and Sunday.

Radio Stations: CHUC AM 1450

Tourist Information: At 212 King Street West, in the Marie Dressler House, the Chamber of Commerce offers tourist information September to June, Monday through Friday 9 A.M. to 5 P.M. and Saturday 9 A.M. to 2 P.M.; July and August, daily 9 A.M. to 5 P.M., 905-372-5831. Ask for the brochure "A Guide to the History and Architectural Heritage of the Town of Cobourg."

A visitor information kiosk operates in July and August in front of Victoria Hall, daily 9 A.M. to 5 P.M.

Step Back in Time: Even if you don't need any information, drop in to see the display of Marie Dressler memorabilia at 212 King Street West. Dressler, a contemporary of Charlie Chaplin and Greta Garbo, starred in early movies and won an Oscar in 1931 for her role in *Min and Bill*. She was born in this cottage and lived here for 17 years until she ran away to join a travelling opera troupe. No charge.

Take a Hike: The Cobourg Conservation Area is the northern anchor for the Cobourg Creek Trail, which begins north of the city and follows the meandering river to its mouth in downtown Cobourg. Turn left at the first lights south of the 401 (Elgin Street). Continue past the Best Western Hotel and the church and then, just past the bridge, turn right into the parking area. The walk to downtown on the trail is 3 kilometres, and best not taken if the spring water-levels are high. No charge.

➤ NORTH

On the Road Again: Division Street in downtown Cobourg leads back to the 401 at IC #474.

#474
Highway 45/
Division Street/Cobourg/
Baltimore

Highway 45 leads north to Hastings and Norwood and the Kawartha Lakes Region. Division Street leads directly south to the business area of Cobourg. Also see IC #472 for Cobourg.

➤ SOUTH
Services:

OPP: Just south on Division Street, 905-372-5421.

Hospital: Cobourg and District General Hospital, 176 Chapel Street (east off Division Street), 905-372-6811.

Roll Back the Clock: The settlement and growth pattern of Cobourg was similar to that of many of the towns and cities of the St. Lawrence and Lake Ontario. Cobourg was founded by United Empire Loyalists in the last years of the 18th century.

Immigration swelled its population after the War of 1812, and the town's continued prosperity from milling, lumbering and a busy harbour led its prominent citizens to believe that it would become the capital of the new province. The elaborate town hall on King Street is the result of that confidence. Tours of Victoria Hall are conducted during July and August, Monday to Friday 2 P.M. or by appointment.

To Market: Continuing a tradition since 1850, Cobourg holds a farmers' market on Saturday mornings May to October in Market Square behind Victoria Hall.

Picnic in the Park: Cobourg's heady prosperity of the mid-1800s did not last. Between the burden of the outrageous construction costs of the town hall, the selection of another town as provincial capital, and a falling population, prospects were bleak until someone discovered that Cobourg air had the second-highest ozone content in the world. Although it sounds like just another fad, the belief in the health benefits of ozone-laden air brought vacationers from all over North America. By the turn of the century, Cobourg had blossomed into a fashionable summer resort. Today the town's lakeshore is home to a sandy beach at Victoria Park, a long pier, a 3-kilometre promenade from the park to the marina building, wading pools and playground equipment.

For Art's Sake: The Art Gallery of Northumberland is located on the third floor of magnificent Victoria Hall at 55 King Street West. Open year-round Tuesday through Friday 9 A.M. to 5 P.M.; Saturday and Sunday 1 P.M. to 5 P.M.; July and August, also Saturday 11 A.M. to 5 P.M., 905-372-0333. No charge.

➤ NORTH
Services:

Take a Hike: In the village of Baltimore, 4 kilometres north of the 401, turn left on Harwood Road. The large mill on the right, Ball's Mill, is the last surviving mill in the area. It was built in 1842 as a carding mill and converted in 1846 to a flour mill. The sign on the large, white frame building reads "The Belle of Baltimore for Bread." Privately owned, the mill is not open to the public. Continue for 0.5 kilometres to Ball's Mill Conservation Area. Steps lead down to a trail along Baltimore Creek. No charge.

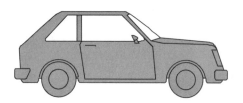

#487
Aird Street/ Northumberland Road 23/ Grafton

Grafton (population 360) is 1 kilometre south of the 401 on Highway 2, midway between Cobourg and Colborne. To the north are the rolling Northumberland Hills.

➤ SOUTH
Services:

Antiques: Grafton is a small crossroads community with a plethora of heritage buildings, a couple of churches, a general store and a number of antique shops. The antique shops are either on Highway 2 or close to it.

Step Back in Time: Drop in at the municipal office for a copy of the brochure "Historical Walking Tour of Grafton." Many of the village buildings date to the mid-1800s and reveal the lakeside town's early prosperity. Three early churches in town have interesting old burial grounds.

The big, white frame house of Eliakim Barnum, 2 kilometres west of Grafton, is said to be one of the finest examples of colonial architecture in Canada. It has been described as representing "the pinnacle of good taste during the Loyalist period." Built in 1819–20, the Barnum House has survived many owners and many internal changes but remains virtually unchanged on the outside. Operated today as the Barnum House Museum, it has been restored to the period 1820–50. Open mid-May to Labour Day, daily 10 A.M. to 4 P.M.; rest of the year 1 P.M. to 4 P.M. Small admission charge.

Take a Hike: Barnum Conservation Area is a natural area located behind the museum. It is open year-round and suitable for hiking. Few facilities. No charge.

➤ NORTH

I N T E R C H A N G E

#497
Percy Street/ Northumberland Road 25/ Big Apple Drive/ Colborne/Castleton

---

The larger Loyalist settlements along Lake Ontario all had one thing in common: each made its bid as the perfect location for the province's capital and each in its own way planned to accommodate the great events associated with the honour. Colborne was no exception—look at its wide main street. Colborne is less than 3 kilometres south of the 401.

➤ SOUTH
Services:

Even though 3,000 pieces of apple pie are served some days at the Big Apple, it is more than a restaurant. Visitors can climb inside the 35-foot-high (10.5 m) apple, visit the gift shop and Brian McFarlane's Hockey Museum, watch the goings-on in the bakery, play miniature golf, try their luck at Bank Shot (basketball), visit the playground, and feed the resident animals. Open daily, summer 8 A.M. to 9 P.M.; winter 8 A.M. to 7 P.M., 905-355-2574.

Newspaper: *Colborne Chronicle*, weekly Wednesdays.

Tourist Information: Seasonal at the Big Apple.

Roll Back the Clock: In East Colborne, the octagonal house at 45 Parliament Street was probably built in response to the theories of American philosopher Orson Fowler, who believed that eight-sided structures were conducive to good health and a sunny disposition. East Colborne is east 2 kilometres on Highway 2 from Percy Street. Turn

north on Parliament Street. See
IC #431 for an octagonal manse
and IC #320 for an octagonal barn.

To Market: A farmers' market takes
place in Colborne Wednesday and
Saturday mornings, May to
October.

For Art's Sake: Check out the
aluminium and marble sculptures
created by the Hoselton clan and
their associates, at Hoselton Studio.
Open daily 9 A.M. to 4 P.M. at
1 Hoselton Drive, 1.4 kilometres
south of the 401, just off Percy
Street, 905-355-3933.

Special Events: On the Victoria
Day weekend in May, the town of
Colborne celebrates spring with
the Apple Blossom Tyme Festival.
Walking tours and hobby and craft
shows are all part of the weekend
festivities.

Off the Beaten Track: Little Lake is
a little-known lake, at least to those
hurtling past on the 401. Take the
first left turn south of the 401 onto
Purdy Road and continue east for
about 7 kilometres. There is public
access on the western edge of the
lake, a short distance up the gravel
road. Little Lake Pavilion serves
lunch and dinner Tuesday through
Sunday from noon till 8 P.M. Casual
food is served at the snack bar,
613-475-0290. Continue east on Little
Lake Road (Purdy Road undergoes a
name change) to Highway 30 and
return to the 401 at IC #509.

➤ NORTH
Services: At 3 kilometres

On the Road Again: Highway 2
east follows the Apple Route to
Brighton past roadside markets and
"pick-your-own" farms.

INTERCHANGE

#509
Highway 30/
Brighton/
Campbellford

You'll find restaurants, antique shops
and accommodation in downtown
Brighton (population 4,300), 5 kilometres south of the 401. Presqu'ile
Provincial Park is another 5 kilometres south.

➤ SOUTH
Services:

OPP: On Young Street at the
northern edge of town, 613-475-1313.
Newspaper: *Brighton Independent*,
weekly on Tuesdays.
Tourist Information: A tourist
information kiosk is open in
downtown Brighton on Main Street
in Memorial Park, mid-May to mid-
October, daily 9 A.M. to 6 P.M.

To Market: On summer Saturday mornings a farmers' market operates on Proctor Street, north of the CIBC.

Step Back in Time: There is a reason for the grand size of Proctor House. Successful merchant and shipping magnate John Proctor built the impressive Italianate house in the 1860s for his family of ten. It has been restored and furnished to depict the lifestyle of the wealthy merchant class of Proctor's time. Proctor House Museum at 96 Young Street is open July and August, Monday to Friday 10 A.M. to 4 P.M., weekends 1 P.M. to 4 P.M. Admission charge, 613-475-2144.

Picnic in the Park: On the way into town, about 3 kilometres south of the 401, tiny Spring Valley Park beside Butler Creek provides picnic tables, barbecues and washrooms. No charge.

If you need more space, the 79-acre (32 ha) Proctor Conservation Area, next to Proctor House Museum, offers picnic tables, washrooms, a hiking/cross-country ski trail, and in winter a toboggan slope. No charge.

Off the Beaten Track: Although Northumberland Brewers on Highway 2, 2 kilometres west of Brighton, is not really off the beaten

---

A Scent from the Past

Brought to Canada as slips tucked in emigrants' baggage, and planted here by early settlers close to their homestead doors, the first Canadian lilacs were a fragrant reminder of home and a talisman against the inevitable strangeness of a new land. When you see a clump growing wild in a meadow, you can assume a pioneer home once stood close by.

The lilac was introduced to England and Europe from Turkey centuries ago. Originally, the shrub's pithy shoots were used to make wind instruments, thus the genus name, *Syringa*, originating from the Greek word for the "pipes of Pan." Easy to propagate, hardy in transit, and requiring little care, the lilac was just too easy and was eventually scorned by elitist gardeners who considered it common and vulgar. French hybrids, developed by Lemoine in the 19th century, and Isabel Preston's creation of hardier varieties in the 1920s at Ottawa's experimental farm, offer today's gardener many lilac choices.

On a good year, when the weather in May has not turned too hot too fast and heavy rains have not weighed down the shrubs, the lilacs growing beside Highway 401 and along fence lines and driveways paint the landscape with a brilliant display of purples, mauves and white. The sideroads along Glen Miller Road north of Trenton (IC #523) and Windmill Point (IC #716 or #721), between Prescott and Johnstown, have spectacular lilac displays in mid to late May.

track, it does produce a rather offbeat product. The shop is open daily, for samples and sales of Scrumpie Cider, an alcoholic cider, 613-475-2143.

Special Events: On the third weekend in September, Brightonians celebrate the current harvest with Applefest, 613-475-APPL.

Further Afield: For miles of sandy beach, boardwalks, forested trails, fishing, an 1840s working lighthouse, interpretive programs and guided walks, continue through town, west on Highway 2 and south on Ontario Street to Presqu'ile Provincial Park. Presqu'ile, almost an island, is an unusual land formation called a tombolo. A limestone island is connected to the mainland peninsula by a sand bar. The 125 nesting bird species and many spring and fall migrants give Presqu'ile its hot-spot status among birders. Tune into 91.7 FM for the current park program (the area of reception is limited), 613-475-2204.

➢ **NORTH**

Antiques: Breakaway Antiques, specializing in furniture, tools, primitives and old postcards, is located 4.5 kilometres north on Highway 30 and west on Guertin Road. Open by chance or appoint-ment, 613-475-2671.

On the Road Again: For a long alternate route back to the 401, pick up County Road 64, east off Prince Edward Drive (the continuation of

Young Street). Continue past the races, go-karts, miniature golf and batting cages of Brighton Speedway Park (613-475-1102) to the swing bridge over the Murray Canal, Kente Fort and the town of Carrying Place (see IC #522). Return to the 401 on Highway 33.

Alternately, follow Highway 2 East and stop in at the Sap Bucket, a gift shop and tearoom (lunch is served till 3:30 P.M.) in Smithfield, 5 kilometres east; store, 613-475-0180; tearoom, 613-475-3636.

#522
Wooler Road/ Northumberland Road 40

Wooler Road south is the beginning of the Loyalist Parkway, a 94-kilometre route from Trenton to Kingston through the area settled by the United Empire Loyalists more than 200 years ago. If you do not have time for the whole route, return to the 401 by any of the north-south highways—Highway 33, Highway 62, Highway 49, or High-way 133. The hamlet of Wooler, 7 kilometres north, has a gas station, a couple of antique shops and a variety store.

➤ SOUTH
Services:

Bargain Hunt: Go south on Wooler Road, cross Highway 2 and continue south on Highway 33, a total of 6.6 kilometres. On Sunday from 10 A.M. to 5 P.M., dealers at Scotty's Market offer a bit of everything, new and old, 613-392-4462. Farther south at Carrying Place, at the junction of Highway 33 and Rednersville Road, O'Hara's Flea Market is also open Saturdays and Sundays, 613-392-0300.

Step Back in Time: The narrow neck of land separating the Bay of Quinte from Lake Ontario was discovered early in Canada's transportation history. Used as a portage route, it eliminated the long voyage around the fingers of Quinte's Isle and became known as Carrying Place. By the time of the War of 1812, it was considered a strategic route. In 1992, Fort Kente was rebuilt on the site of a fort originally built in 1813 to secure this route. Each year at the fort, on the third weekend in July, canoe races, military encampments and historical reenactments celebrate the history of Ontario's oldest road. To get there, turn left at County Road 64, 8.5 kilometres south of the 401. Continue west for 2 kilometres, 613-394-2313.

When the Murray Canal was built in the 1880s to provide a water route where once only a portage had been possible, the peninsula of Prince Edward County became an island. At each end of the canal, swing bridges accommodate both road and boat traffic. The eastern entrance of the Murray Canal is located 7.5 kilometres south of the 401 on Highway 33. Picnic areas and trails.

➤ NORTH
Services:

On the Road Again: Follow Highway 33 east into Trenton. Watch for the historic marker at Dufferin Street and Shuter Street, and turn left onto Shuter. A stone cairn commemorates Trenton's place in the history of the film world. In a building now occupied by Bayside Dyeing & Finishing Co. Ltd. on Film Street, international movie stars starred in movies produced here between 1917 and 1934. The first Carry On movie, *Carry On Sergeant*, was filmed here. It flopped at the box office.

#525
Highway 33/
Trenton/Frankford

To the south, Highway 33 is the first of two exits leading to downtown Trenton (population 16,500). The western gateway to the Loyalist Parkway and Quinte's Isle, Trenton is located on the Bay of Quinte at the mouth of the Trent River. Six kilometres to the north, Thomas Bata built the company town of Batawa to accommodate workers at his Bata Shoe Company.

➤ SOUTH
Services:

Downtown Trenton

Hospital: Trenton Memorial Hospital, 242 King Street, 613-392-2541.

Newspaper: *Trentonian*, published Monday, Wednesday, Friday.
Radio Station: CJTN AM1270
Tourist Information: The Chamber of Commerce at 97 Front Street is open year-round, Monday through Friday from 9 A.M. to 5 P.M., 613-392-7635. The Heritage Caboose in the parking lot at 97 Front Street is open seasonally.
To Market: A farmers' market is held in the parking lot near the Chamber of Commerce offices on Front Street on Tuesday, Thursday, and Saturday mornings from April through October.
Trent–Severn Waterway: Originally designed to facilitate the booming trade of the 19th century, the Trent–Severn Waterway now carries pleasure boaters through 44 locks and along 386 kilometres of rivers, lakes and canals from Lake Ontario to Georgian Bay. The system begins in Trenton where the Trent River spills into Lake Ontario. Lock One is just south on Highway 33 on the west side of the river. A visitor centre provides information and sells souvenirs. Although the park area around the locks is accessible year-round for picnics, the locks operate only from mid-May till mid-October. No charge for picnicking.
Picnic in the Park: Farther south along the Trent River, a 10-acre (4 ha) band of green, the Trenton Greenbelt, has public picnic facilities and trails.
Off the Beaten Track: Where Highway 33 ends, in downtown Trenton, take the right arm of the Y, Division Street. Turn right at King Street, right again at Dufferin Street and then left at Spring Street.

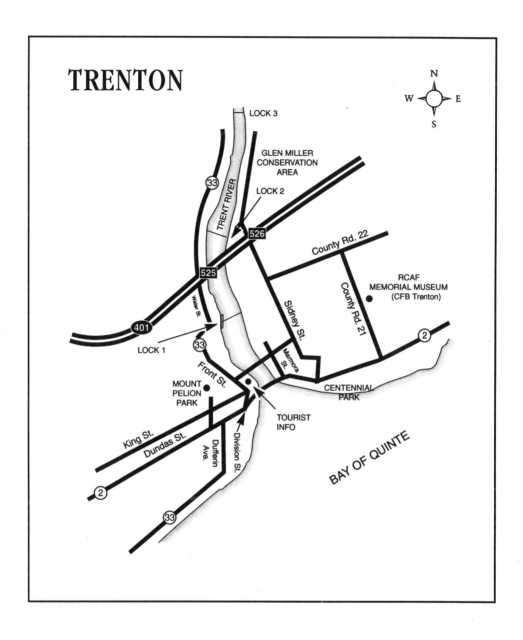

TRENTON

Continue on Spring for one more block to MacLellan Street. The large, redbrick building on Spring Street, the Dufferin Centre, was built in 1913 as a public school. Directly behind the school at the end of MacLellan Street, Mount Pelion rises 445 feet (135 m). The panorama of the Bay of Quinte from the summit is impressive. Audio tapes describing the history of the area and the view from the tower are available at the

Trenton Chamber of Commerce at 97 Front Street. Picnic tables. Parking.

➤ NORTH
Services:

On the Road Again: From Highway 33 north, cross the Trent River at Glen Miller and return to the 401 via Glen Miller Road, IC #526. To the south, the bridge at the junction of Division and Front Streets crosses the Trent River. Sidney Street, the southern continuation of Glen Miller Road, returns to the 401 at IC #526.

INTERCHANGE

#526
Glen Miller Road/ Trenton/ CFB Trenton

Glen Miller Road runs parallel to the Trent River and the Trent–Severn Waterway, north of the 401. To the south, Sidney Street bisects eastern Trenton. See also IC #525 for Trenton.

➤ SOUTH
Services:

Factory Outlets: *Bata Shoe Outlet*, 400 Sidney Street, shoes for all. Open Monday through Thursday 9:30 A.M. to 6 P.M.; Friday 9:30 A.M. to 9 P.M.; Saturday 9:30 A.M. to 5 P.M., 613-392-0858. *Vagden Mill Store*, 390 Sidney Street, for socks, some sweaters and towels. Open Monday through Saturday 9:30 A.M. to 5 P.M., 613-392-9391.

Clearly Canadian: The RCAF Memorial Museum combines indoor exhibits on the force's history and an outdoor Air Park displaying an extensive collection of heritage and current aircraft. Take County Road 22 left off Sidney Street just south of the 401 and continue for 1.5 kilometres to County Road 21. The museum is located on the base, 2 kilometres south. Open Monday through Thursday 10 A.M. to 5 P.M. and 6 P.M. to 8 P.M.; Friday, Saturday and Sunday 10 A.M. to 5 P.M., 613-965-2208 or 965-2140. No charge.

➤ NORTH
Services:

 Sunoco

Say Cheese: At the Riverside Cheese Factory on Riverside Drive (the first

Glen Miller Boulder

Geologists refer to it as an erratic, but anyone who stands beside the house-size boulder at Glen Miller considers it stable, and big! No one has actually put it on the scales, but it is estimated to weigh as much as 1,000 tons. That's 2 million pounds, or 910,000 kilograms or 143,000 stone—colossal by any measure. When the last glaciers retreated from the area 20,000 years ago, they dropped their load as they melted. Pebbles, rocks and boulders picked up along the way were left far from their parent bedrock. The Glen Miller Boulder, north of Trenton, is one of the largest known erratics in Southeastern Ontario, and to give it some measure of protection (surely not from theft!) the government has designated the rock and the surrounding acre of land an Area of Natural Scientific Interest. In 1994, the private land on the west side of the Trent River on which it rests went on the market as part of an estate sale and its future accessibility is unknown.

street to the west) fresh curds and other dairy products are available daily. The Riverside Dairy delivered milk in Trenton with a horse and wagon until 1964. Open Monday through Wednesday 8 A.M. to 6 P.M.; Thursday and Friday 8 A.M. to 8 P.M.; Saturday 8 A.M. to 6 P.M.; Sunday 9:30 A.M. to 5 P.M. Winter hours vary, 613-392-6762.

Picnic in the Park: In a quiet oasis between the Trent River and Glen Miller Road, only 1 kilometre north of the 401, Glen Miller Conservation Area provides a quiet picnic spot. Outdoor washrooms and picnic tables. No charge.

Trent–Severn Waterway: The public viewing area for Lock Two is on the east side of the river. Turn left at the sign for Lock Two, before the Glen Miller Conservation Area, and follow the road as it turns back south along the river. Return to Glen Miller Road and continue north another kilometre to Lock Three. Picnic facilities, information and washrooms. In the first six locks covering the 10-kilometre stretch from Trenton, north to Frankford, boats climb 115 feet (35 m). The locks usually open for traffic in mid-May and close by mid-October.

Season's Best: In late May, lilacs bloom in profusion along Glen Miller Road and the nearby sideroads. The apparent random locations of the lilac bushes mark the sites of early farmhouses.

On the Road Again: It's a long stretch from this interchange to the next. As an alternate route through

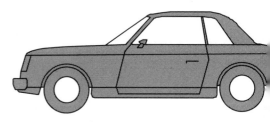

the countryside, take County Road 22 east for 12 kilometres to Wallbridge Road and IC #538. For a lakeside drive, follow Highway 2 east through the Canadian Forces Base to hook up with Wallbridge Road just beyond Quinte Conservation Area. Note the elaborate gates at the official entrance to the base. In recognition of the thousands of airmen trained here for the Second World War, the governments of Great Britain, Australia and New Zealand in 1949 presented the Royal Canadian Air Force with these Memorial Gates. The coats of arms of Canada and Great Britain decorate the centre gates and those of Australia and New Zealand are featured on the side pedestrian gates.

INTERCHANGE

#538
Wallbridge Road/ Loyalist Road/Stirling

Wallbridge Road leads south to the Bay of Quinte and Highway 2. To the north, rural Ontario stretches to Stirling, Marmora and Madoc.

➤ SOUTH
Services:

OPP: South on Wallbridge Road, 613-968-6495.

Take a Hike: Quinte Conservation Area at Highway 2 and Wallbridge Road (4.5 kilometres south of the 401) offers a variety of activities. In the park area south of Highway 2, you can picnic, barbeque, swim in the Bay of Quinte, and fish in nearby Potter Creek. North of Highway 2, 5 kilometres of hiking and ski trails wander around overgrown hedgerows and through grassy fields.

The Moira River Conservation Authority's offices are located in the old Potter farmhouse on the property. No charge.

➤ NORTH
Services:

On the Road Again: Take either Moira Road or Highway 2 east to Belleville and return to the 401 via Highway 62, IC #543 or Highway 37, IC #544.

INTERCHANGE

#543
Highway 62/
Belleville/Madoc
★

Highway 62 leads north to the cottage country of Madoc and Bancroft. To the south, Highway 62, which becomes North Front Street, is the most westerly of the two exits into Belleville and the one with a profusion of services close to the 401. Much of Belleville's 19th-century prosperity can be traced to the lumbering and milling industries and to Ontario's first gold strike at Eldorado, 50 kilometres north. City politicians, confident of the city's prospects, petitioned Queen Victoria to make Belleville the capital of Canada. The drive to downtown Belleville, 3.5 kilometres south, might take as long as 10 minutes on a busy weekday.

➤ SOUTH

Services:

Quinte Mall (115 stores)
OPP: Just south of the 401 off North Front Street, 613-968-5547.
Newspaper: *The Intelligencer*, daily.
Radio Station: CIGL 97.1 FM, CJBQ 800 AM, CJOJ 95.5 FM
Tourist Information: The Belleville and District Chamber of Commerce provides tourist information at 5 Moira Street East (North Front Street and Moira Street) Monday to Friday 9 A.M. to 5 P.M., 613-962-4597.

Roll Back the Clock: The house at 114 Bridge Street was once the home of pioneer writer Susanna Moodie. In her autobiographical work, *Life in the Clearings*, she described Belleville in 1840 as "an insignificant, dirty-looking place," but was quick to add that in the following 12 years, Belleville had experienced "an almost miraculous change. It has more than doubled its dimensions and its population has increased to upwards of 4,500 souls. Handsome commodious stores, filled with expensive goods from the mother country and the States, have risen in the place of the small dark frame buildings; and large hotels have jostled into obscurity the low taverns and groceries that once formed the only places of entertainment." Belleville's prosperity had begun.

Susanna Moodie came from an extraordinarily literary family. Her sister Catharine Parr Traill is best known for *The Backwoods of Canada*, and her brother Samuel Strickland

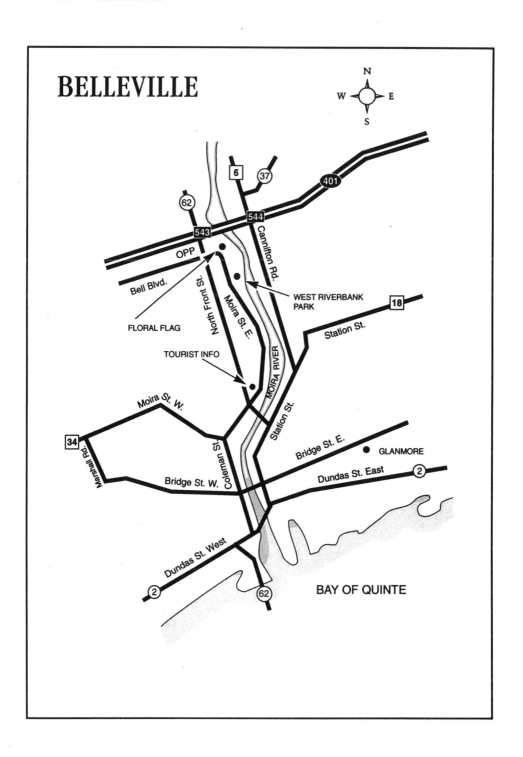

BELLEVILLE

wrote his pioneering account in *Twenty-seven Years in Canada West*. Moodie lived with her husband for 25 years in the fieldstone cottage at 114 Bridge Street.

To Market: A farmers' market takes place Tuesday, Thursday and Saturday mornings behind the city hall on Pinnacle Street. Seasonal.

Picnic in the Park: Turn left on Bell Boulevard and continue east to the large, well-developed West Riverbank Park. Picnic, swimming, canteen and washroom facilities are available on the banks of the Moira River. See IC #544 for the eastern section of the park.

Say Cheese: The turreted castle, west about 1 kilometre on Bell Boulevard, is fit for a dairy queen. Milkshakes, ice cream, cheese and curds are sold in the fantasy surroundings of Reid's Dairy. Open Monday through Wednesday and Saturday 8 A.M. to 8 P.M.; Thursday and Friday till 9:30 P.M.; Sunday 9 A.M. to 8 P.M., 613-967-1970.

➤ **NORTH**
Services:

Patriotic Plantings

Each spring, thousands of plants in the City of Belleville's greenhouses transform the south embankment just east of Highway 62 into a gigantic floral flag. The flag project, begun in 1990, continues each year with financial support from the local Veteran's Council and a lot of labour from the city's parks department. Although there have been some close calls when late spring frosts threatened the tender new plantings, the flag has always survived to claim rave reviews from passing motorists.

Usually the flag depicted is the red maple leaf, adopted as Canada's flag in February 1965. It is described as "A red flag of the proportions two by length and one by width...containing in its centre a white square the width of the flag, with a single red maple leaf centred therein."

For a flag photo opportunity, exit at Highway 62 south (IC #543), turn left at Bell Boulevard and left again at North Park Street. From mid-September till mid-October, the City showcases plantings of 10,000 chrysanthemums just south of the flag.

Factory Outlet: Vagden Socks in the Somerville Centre, north 2 kilometres on Highway 62, is another outlet for the factory in Trenton. Open Monday through Wednesday and Saturday 9:30 A.M. to 5:30 P.M.; Thursday and Friday 9 A.M. to 9 P.M., Sunday 11 A.M. to 5 P.M. 613-966-7725.
On the Road Again: Highway 62 to downtown Belleville brings you down the west side of the Moira River. To pick up Highway 37 to return north to IC #544, take Dundas Street east from downtown or Station Street from midtown.

#544
Highway 37/
Belleville/Tweed

Highway 37 leads north to the pretty town of Tweed (36 kilometres) and south to Belleville.

➤ SOUTH
Services:

All services in downtown Belleville via Dundas Street.

Hospital: Belleville General Hospital, 265 Dundas Street East, 613-969-7400.
Picnic in the Park: Highway 37 south follows the meandering Moira River to downtown Belleville and the Bay of Quinte. Ultimately named for

Sir John Rawdon, the Earl of Moira, the river has had numerous name changes, revealing the area's history. The French called it Ohate, or Barbu (Catfish) River. The Loyalists stayed with the Indian-sounding Sagonash-kokan. Later it was known as Single-ton Creek and then Meyer's Creek. Just south of the 401, Riverside Park provides picnic tables along the river's edge. See IC #543 for the western portion of the park.
Step Back in Time: It's worth the drive into town for a view of Glanmore, the Hastings County Museum at 257 Bridge Street East. The mansion, built in 1883 in a soaring Italianate design, with a mansard roof and every imaginable Victorian architectural extreme, displays artefacts typical of upper-class, turn-of-the-century life. Victorian tea is served during July and August. Open June through August, Tuesday through Friday 10 A.M. to 4:30 P.M.; Saturday and Sunday 1 P.M. to 4:30 P.M.; September through May, Tuesday through Sunday 1 P.M. to 4:30 P.M. Admission charge, 613-962-2329.

➤ NORTH
Services:

No services until the Hollyrood Beef House (5 kilometres north), open daily at 7 A.M. for breakfast until at least 9 P.M. Sunday through Thursday and until 11 P.M. Friday and Saturday. 613-967-8910.
On the Road Again: Highway 2 east and County Road 18 both lead to Shannonville Road IC #556.

INTERCHANGE

#556
Shannonville Road/
Hastings Road 7/
Shannonville

➤ SOUTH

➤ NORTH

On the Road Again: For the scenic route follow Shannonville Road south 2.5 kilometres to Highway 2, turn left on Highway 2 and then make a quick right at York Road. York Road continues for 12 kilometres through Tyendinaga Mohawk Territory to Highway 49. See IC #566 for services at Highway 49 and Highway 2 east.

INTERCHANGE

#566
Highway 49/
Marysville Road/
Tyendinaga/Picton

Highway 49 leads south through the Tyendinaga Mohawk Territory and crosses the Bay of Quinte to Prince Edward County and Picton.

➤ SOUTH
Services:

 Sunoco

At the junction of Highway 49 and Highway 2 east, 5 kilometres south

For Art's Sake: On Highway 49 south, a number of shops sell native art and crafts. At Native Renaissance II, at the junction of Highway 49 and Highway 2 east, crafts are for sale on the ground floor and prints, paintings and sculptures on the second floor. A 125-foot (38 m) mural transforms the building's outside wall into an ancient native village. Open May 1 to Labour Day, daily 9 A.M. to 9 P.M. Off-season hours are shorter, 613-396-3255.

Play Awhile: Turn right at Highway 2 west and continue for 4 kilometres to Shannonville Motorsport Park. Test your skill on the track in a go-kart. Spectator events. Open all year; seasonal hours, 613-969-1906.

Step Back in Time: On a hill overlooking the Bay of Quinte, under the shade of ancient oaks, Oronhyatekha, a renowned Mohawk chief, is buried in the cemetery of the Anglican Christ Church. The church, although damaged by fire in 1906, appears virtually unchanged from its construction in 1843. At the junction of Highway 49 and Highway 2 east, turn left and continue on Highway 2 for about 1 kilometre before turning right at the sign. The church, with its magnificent Gothic tower, can be seen to the south.

Special Events: On the third Sunday in May, the people of the territory gather in full ceremonial dress at the chapel and at Tsitkerhedodon Park to reenact the 1784 landing of the Mohawks. Communion silver presented to the Mohawks by Queen Anne in 1711 is brought out of the vault for viewing; traditional foods are served and visitors are welcome. Tsitkerhedodon Park is on Bayshore Road, south of Highway 2. Follow the signs for the Mohawk Landing historic marker.

On the second weekend in August, the territory hosts a traditional powwow—a 2-day event highlighting traditional native crafts, music and food, 613-396-3424.

Fair Days: On the first weekend after Labour Day in September, the Tyendinaga Territory holds a fall fair in the Mohawk Fairgrounds. The fair, a tradition for more than 100 years, combines agricultural contests with traditional native foods, crafts and games. There may be a few games of lacrosse. Follow Highway 49 south and turn right opposite Highway 2 east. The fairgrounds are located about 3 kilometres west. Rumour has it that Mrs. Herb's Coffee Shop, across from the community centre, serves great food, 613-962-0938.

➤ NORTH

On the Road Again: It is a short drive along Bayshore Road or Highway 2 east to Deseronto.

Red-winged Blackbird

Every marsh seems to support at least one pair of red-winged blackbirds. In spring, you can see the male in among the clumps of roadside cattails, with his head thrown back, his wings spread and his tail bobbing as he sings his heart out for the drab female. The disappearance of either one deep into last year's cattail foliage indicates nest-building or nest-tending duties. Mature males are always glossy black with some shoulder red, orange or yellow, and if the scarlet patch is not visible, it is probably concealed by other wing feathers. The females are nondescript brown with well-defined streaks on the underside. The red-winged blackbird arrives early to Southern Ontario, a welcome harbinger of spring.

#570
Deseronto Road/
Deseronto

North, you will find rural country-side. Five kilometres south, the town of Deseronto, with a population of fewer than 2,000, is a shadow of its former self. The town was named for Captain John Deserontoyou, leader of the band of 60 or 70 Mohawks who first landed on the shores of the Bay of Quinte in 1784. By 1890, the town was the centre of the entrepreneurial empire of H.B. Rathburn, whose sawmills, flour mills, factories and stores employed as many as 5,000 people. The fine brick houses and massive old buildings, some still bearing the faded traces of painted advertisements, hint of those prosperous times.

➤ **SOUTH**
Services: In Deseronto, 5 kilometres

➤ **NORTH**

On the Road Again: The drive on Highway 2 beside the Bay leads you past many fine mansions on the western edge of Napanee.

INTERCHANGE

#579
Highway 41/
Napanee/Kaladar

Highway 41 exits on the west side of the Napanee River and leads to downtown Napanee, 2 kilometres south. Napanee is a Loyalist town that was settled in 1786 by hardy pioneers and ambitious entrepreneurs who were attracted to the site by the promise of water power from Appanea Falls. The Gibbard Furniture Company drew on that early power and has remained in business in virtually the same location beside the river since 1835. Along Highway 2 west the spacious properties and grand heritage homes attest to the town's early prosperity. See IC #582 for additional Napanee information.

➤ **SOUTH**
Services:

Napanee Mall (26 stores)

OPP: Just south of the 401, 613-354-3369.

Hospital: Lennox and Addington County General Hospital, 8 Park Drive, 613-354-3301.

Newspaper: *Napanee Beaver*, weekly on Wednesdays.

Tourist Information: A seasonal information kiosk operates on the edge of the Napanee Mall.

Step Back in Time: Old Napanee is well preserved in the former county jail, now the Lennox and Addington County Museum and Archives, located at 97 Thomas Street East. Open Monday to Friday noon to 4:30 P.M.; Sundays (except November to March) 1 P.M. to 4:30 P.M. Closed holidays, 613-354-3027.

Picnic in the Park: Follow Highway 41 (Centre Street) to Dundas Street (Highway 2) and continue over the Centre Street Bridge. Turn right on Victoria Avenue and into the Napanee Conservation Area on the banks of the Napanee River. A boardwalk extends from the conservation area to Springside Park (see IC #582). Picnic facilities, washrooms. No charge. Park here. It is only a short walk back to the shopping area along Dundas Street.

➤ NORTH
Services:

On the Road Again: From the south, continue east on Dundas Street and then north on William Street along the east side of the river to return to the 401 via IC #582.

INTERCHANGE

#582
Palace Road/ Newburgh/Napanee

Whether you go north or south at this exit, the Napanee River is the main attraction. To the north along the river are the towns of Strathcona, Newburgh and Camden East. To the south, William Street follows the river to the falls in downtown Napanee.

➤ SOUTH
Services:

All services in downtown Napanee on Dundas Street.

The Royal Coachman Restaurant is less than 1 kilometre east on Highway 2. Open for lunch daily 11:30 A.M. to 1:30 P.M. and for dinner from 5 P.M., 613-354-9124.

Picnic in the Park: West on Highway 2, at the foot of William Street, Springside Park follows the fall of the river. A boardwalk extends from this picturesque park to the Napanee Conservation Area (see IC #579). Picnic tables, walking path, fishing. No charge.

Step Back in Time: On the west bank of the river, north of Dundas Street, the Allan Macpherson House, home of one of 19th-century Napanee's leading citizens, is restored to the 1820–40 period. Macpherson was the mill operator, store owner, postmaster and magistrate. He included in the design of his house two features seldom seen today—the absence of an exterior door handle on the front door to symbolize the hospitality of the owner who graciously opened the door for all his guests; and equally attractive facades on both the street side and the river side of the house. Open from Victoria Day through Thanksgiving, weekends only, 1 P.M. to 5 P.M.

➢ NORTH
Services: None till the Newburgh turn, 7.5 kilometres

Off the Beaten Track: Substantial banks along both sides of the Napanee River create a deep valley in which the town of Newburgh nestles. Its former name, The Hollow, was appropriate. There are no museums, no tourist attractions and few services, but the town has wonderful old stone buildings, ruins of a mill beside the falls (on Earl Street), and a picturesque century-old graveyard (at the top of Earl Street). Turn left off County Road 1, 7.5 kilometres north of the 401.

On the Road Again: Highway 2 east dips a bit south on the way to Camden Road IC #593 and will add a few kilometres to your trip. Even if you decide to return to the 401 on William Street, drive just a bit east on Highway 2 if you want to see an impressive rock cut made when the road was built.

#593
Highway 133/
Camden East Road/
Millhaven/Camden East

Millhaven is 10 kilometres south of the 401 on Highway 133, a rural route as far as Lake Ontario. To the north is the village of Camden East, former home of *Harrowsmith* magazine.

➢ SOUTH

➢ NORTH
Services: None until Camden East, 7.2 kilometres

Roll Back the Clock: As the early Loyalist settlers took up the lots near the shores of the St. Lawrence River and Lake Ontario, latecomers were obliged to choose sites farther inland. Settlers preferred lots beside rivers, not only for the power the rivers generated but also for easier transportation. Camden East is one of a string of towns founded on the Napanee River by later settlers. The industry of the 19th century is long gone and the area is now largely residential, but many of the old stone homes have survived.

On the Road Again: Highway 2 east rolls through more of rural Ontario to Odessa.

#599
Wilton Road/ Amherstview/Odessa/ Yarker

Wilton Road leads north to a number of small towns, the first of which is the farming hamlet of Wilton. To the south, turn left at the first lights (Highway 2) to reach the village of Odessa, a former stop on an old stagecoach route. The town was named in 1854 to commemorate a battle of the Crimean War fought in the Russian port of Odessa.

➤ SOUTH
Services:

Picnic in the Park: The Babcock Mill has been restored to operational status and, until recently, opened in the summer months to demonstrate basket-making. Although township cutbacks have kept the mill closed since the end of the 1993 season, the park around the 1856 limestone mill and beside the creek is still a great picnic spot. Go west on Highway 2, and just over the bridge turn left on Bridge Street (1.5 kilometres from the 401).

Special Events: The Odessa Antique Show & Sale, a large outdoor show, is held each year on the second weekend of August at the Odessa fairgrounds. There is a hefty admission charge for "early birds" who enter on Saturday at 2 P.M.; in return they get first crack at the best treasures. Otherwise the show is open Sunday 7 A.M. to 4 P.M. Admission charge, 613-283-1168.

➤ NORTH

There is so little traffic in Wilton (4 kilometres north of the 401, turn right and go another kilometre east) that a turtle can safely cross the main street. Although the farming economy is less vigorous than in earlier times, a feed mill still operates here, in the same location as it has for generations.

Say Cheese: The Wilton Cheese Factory is open daily 10 A.M. to 5 P.M. Curds available. 613-386-7314.

For Art's Sake: In the 1855 lime-stone schoolhouse in town, decorative and functional porcelain and stoneware are created and offered for sale. Wilton Pottery is open April through December, Tuesday through Saturday 10 A.M. to 5 P.M.; Sunday noon to 5 P.M., 613-386-3400.

INTERCHANGE

611
Highway 38/
Harrowsmith/
Sharbot Lake

Highway 38 north passes through a number of small towns and lake country to connect with Highway 7 at Sharbot Lake, 67 kilometres to the north. To the south, the highway skirts the western edge of greater Kingston.

➤ SOUTH
Services:

At Highway 2, 3 kilometres

At Cataraqui Town Centre (100-plus stores), 4 kilometres

At Highway 33, 6 kilometres

  Burger King

OPP: Just north of Highway 2, east on O'Connor Drive, 613-384-2400.
Antiques: Kingston Antique Centre, 1257 Midland Avenue. For this multi-dealer shop, turn right on Midland Avenue just below the 401. Open daily 11 A.M. to 5 P.M., 613-384-1850.

➤ NORTH

Red-tailed Hawk

Red-tailed hawks are daytime hunters; they perch on trees or fence posts to look for mice and snakes. Face on, the big, thick-set birds (up to 25 inches, or 63 cm, in height) appear light in colour but from the back they appear a dark, greyish brown. The rusty-coloured, blunt tail is most easily seen while the bird is in flight. A red-tailed hawk sailing in large circles high in the sky presents a silhouette of a stout body with short wings and a broad, rounded tail. Don't confuse it with the larger, blacker and less chunky turkey vulture. Red-tails do not appear to fear thundering traffic, so you can often spot them close to the highway. Look for a dark silhouette high in a tree or on a lower limb. My record count of red-tails happened on a fall day as I drove from Toronto to Windsor—17 on one side of the highway!

INTERCHANGE

#613
Sydenham Road/ Kingston/ Sydenham

Sydenham Road is the most western of the five exits into Kingston. First settled in 1673 by the French, Kingston ranks as the tenth-oldest city in North America. Its characteristic limestone buildings appear in many guises, from small, modest square homes to the imposing city hall, built to house Canada's parliament but never used as such. At Queen's University, modern limestone structures and heritage buildings dating to the mid-1800s stand side-by-side.

➤ SOUTH
Services:

At Highway 2, 2.5 kilometres

Step Back in Time: Sydenham Road could be called Cemetery Road. Pass all the cemeteries on the left and the right and almost at Highway 2 take the left turn indicated for the Cataraqui Cemetery. Sir John A. Macdonald, one of the Fathers of Confederation and the first prime minister of Canada, is buried here. The road through the cemetery curves past stately pine trees and emerges north on Sydenham Road. The limestone schoolhouse near the entrance to the cemetery was one of the earliest buildings in the area.

➤ NORTH

On the Road Again: For a slow route into downtown Kingston, take Highway 2 east (becomes Princess Street).

INTERCHANGE

#615
Sir John A. Macdonald Boulevard/ Kingston

Sir John A. Macdonald Boulevard is a fairly new exit off the 401. It leads only south.

➤ SOUTH
Services: At Highway 2, 3 kilometres

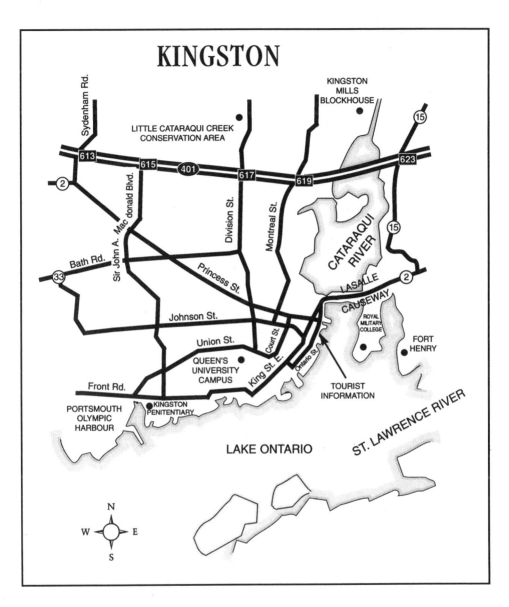

 Holiday Inn

Kingston Centre (90-plus stores)

Clearly Canadian: Just south of the 401, take a quick look to the right before crossing over the bridge. You should be able to see the construction work of a family of beavers living here in the marsh.

Take a Tour: 1000 Island boat tours operate from the Olympic Harbour at Portsmouth. The harbour, which was constructed for the sailing events of the 1976 Montreal Olympics, has since been used for international events. To reach the harbour, drive 6 kilometres south on Sir John A. Macdonald Boulevard and turn right on Front Road. It is about a 10-minute drive. Canada's maximum security prison, the Kingston Penitentiary, looms massive and grey over the harbour.

Step Back in Time: The Correctional Service of Canada Museum, located at 555 King Street West directly across from the Kingston Penitentiary, documents 150 years of Canada's penal system and displays escape paraphernalia and early punishment equipment. Open mid-May to Labour Day, Wednesday through Friday 9 A.M. to 4 P.M.; Saturday and Sunday 10 A.M. to 4 P.M., 613-545-8686.

On the Road Again: Union Street to the east leads to the Queen's University campus. Front Road East becomes King Street East and leads to downtown and the waterfront area.

INTERCHANGE

#617
Division Street/
Kingston
★

Division Street south is the main service route into Kingston, the Limestone City. Take this exit if you need something. To the north the historical Perth Road leads to the village of Westport and eventually to the town of Perth.

➤ SOUTH
Services:

Kingslake Plaza

Hospital: Kingston General Hospital, 76 Stuart Street (south of Queen's), general enquiries 613-548-3232, emergency 613-548-2333.

Newspaper: *Kingston Whig-Standard*, daily.

Radio Stations: CFFX AM 960, CFMK FM 98.3, CFLY FM 98.3

Factory Outlet: Liz Clairborne Outlet Store, ladies' fashions and accessories, some men's wear, 1201 Division Street, Kingslake Plaza, directly off the 401 on the left. Open Monday through Wednesday and Saturday 10 A.M. to 6 P.M.; Thursday and Friday 10 A.M. to 9 P.M.; Sunday noon to 5 P.M., 613-547-1441.

Take a Tour: Queen's University, founded in 1841, is about a 10-minute drive from the 401. Follow Division Street south to Union Street. The campus comprises an area south to the lake and east and west of University Avenue for a half-a-dozen blocks. Call 613-545-2217 weekdays for information on tours.

Step Back in Time: Kingston's long history and rich heritage are well preserved in the many museums and historic sites in the city. The International Ice Hockey Federation Museum, on the corner of Alfred Street and York Street, is within easy reach of the 401. The museum displays memorabilia from the sport's organized beginnings on Kingston's icy harbour in 1886 to today's professional teams. Take Concession Street west off Division Street and turn south on Alfred Street. Open mid-June through September, daily 10 A.M. to 5 P.M. Souvenir shop. Admission charge, 613-544-2355.

➤ NORTH

Take a Hike: Little Cataraqui Creek Conservation Area, an area of wetland and woods 2 kilometres north on Perth Road, takes its name from the early native settlement of Cataraqui, later known as Fort Frontenac and today as Kingston. Picnic, hiking, fishing facilities. A natural skating rink on the reservoir is maintained when winter conditions permit. You can see maple syrup being made here in the spring. Admission charge.

On the Road Again: Montreal Street (IC #617) is easily accessed from any of the east/west streets.

#619 Montreal Street/Kingston

If your needs are immediate, take Division Street, IC #617. If you have a bit of time, take this exit and find services in historic downtown Kingston. The drive south on Montreal Street to downtown will take about 10 minutes, depending on the traffic.

➤ SOUTH

Services:

All services in downtown Kingston.

Hospital: Hotel Dieu Hospital, 166 Brock Street, general inquiries 613-544-3310, emergency 613-546-1240.

Tourist Information: Information is available year-round at the stone railway station built in 1885 at 209 Ontario Street. Ask for information on the self-guided walking tour for downtown Kingston. Thousand Islands boat tours can be booked here. Open year-round. From the end of June to Labour Day, daily 8:30 A.M. to 8:30 P.M. The rest of the year, hours vary, 613-548-4415.

To Market: Year-round on Tuesday, Thursday and Saturday 6 A.M. to 6 P.M., in the area behind the city hall, a farmers' market offers fresh produce and crafts from the surrounding communities. On Sunday morning from April through October, an antique market moves into the same space.

Step Back in Time: Many aspects of Kingston's well-documented past can be explored in the city's wealth of museums. South on Montreal Street, watch for the crenellated tower of the armouries of the Princess of Wales' Own Regiment. Ride the Confederation Tour Train, departing from 209 Ontario Street. Learn a lesson at the Frontenac County Schools Museum at 559 Bagot Street. Tour the *Alexander Henry*, docked next to the Marine Museum of the Great Lakes at 55 Ontario Street.

➤ NORTH

Off the Beaten Track: Kingston Mills Blockhouse, strategically perched on a rocky outcrop at the first lock station of the Rideau Canal, is a perfect picnic spot. The Rideau Canal, built after the War of 1812 to secure a military supply route independent of the vulnerable St. Lawrence River, has been in continuous use for longer than 150 years—first as a commercial artery and in this century as a recreational waterway. Picnic, barbecue and washroom facilities. The Blockhouse is open June 1 through Labour Day, daily 9 A.M. to 4 P.M. The visitor centre is open mid-May to mid-October during lock operating hours.

No charge. Go north on Montreal Road 1.2 kilometres and turn right. The blockhouse and locks are 2 kilometres east.

On the Road Again: From the Kingston Mills Blockhouse continue east for 2 kilometres to Highway 15 and south another 2 kilometres to the 401. From downtown Kingston follow Ontario Street north until it merges with the Lasalle Causeway and becomes Highway 2. Follow Highway 2 past the Royal Military College and Fort Henry to Highway 15 and return to the 401 at IC #623.

INTERCHANGE

#623 Highway 15/ Kingston/ Smiths Falls/ Ottawa

Highway 15 south, the most easterly of the Kingston exits, takes you to Canada's military past, present and future. CFB Kingston is on the right as you travel south. Fort Henry and the Royal Military College are just to the west off Highway 2, and Vimy Barracks is east on Highway 2. To the north, Highway 15 leads to the nation's capital, Ottawa. For further information on Kingston, refer to IC #613, IC #615, IC #617 and IC #619.

➤ SOUTH
Services:

Step Back in Time: History lives at Fort Henry! Built on a cliff at the entrance to the St. Lawrence River as a defence against future attacks from the Americans after the War of 1812, Fort Henry has the distinction of never having fired a shot in battle. By the time the fort was completed in 1836, at great expense to Britain, the American threat had lessened. Now, college students, as members of the Fort Henry Guard, reenact 19th-century garrison life and perform in parades and drills. Open Victoria Day to Thanksgiving, daily 10 A.M. to 5 P.M. Take Highway 15 south to Highway 2 and turn right, a total of 8 kilometres from the 401. Admission charge, 613-542-7388.

Clearly Canadian: At the Royal Military College, located between Fort Henry and Kingston, the officers of tomorrow pursue military and academic studies. A museum housed in a Martello tower at the site's original fort, Fort Frederick, traces the college's history. The grounds are open to the public, but no buildings other than the museum allow public access. Open late June

through Labour Day, daily 10 A.M. to 5 P.M. Donations accepted, 613-541-6000.

➤ NORTH
Services:

The Rideau Canal: As many as four thousand men may have died of disease or injury during the building of the Rideau Canal from 1826 to 1832. Considered an amazing engineering feat for its time, the Rideau Canal climbs up and over Canadian Shield granite, linking lakes, rivers and narrows through 47 locks on its 192-kilometre route to Ottawa. The last locks at the mouth of the Cataraqui River, and the Kingston Mills Blockhouse can be reached from this exit or the previous one, IC #619. To reach these locks from Highway 15, travel 1.5 kilometres north, turn left and continue for 2 kilometres. Depending on your direction of travel, use one exit to reach the locks and return to the 401 by the other one. See IC #619 for museum times and facilities. A great picnic spot.

On the Road Again: On Highway 2, 1.7 kilometres east of Highway 15, at the rear of the Forde Building in Vimy Barracks, the Canadian Forces Communications and Electronics Museum documents military communication methods from early radios to satellites. Open year-round weekdays 8 A.M. to 4 P.M. Also, summer weekends 10 A.M. to 4 P.M. No charge. New quarters for the museum, on the north side of Highway 2 across from Vimy Gate, should be ready in 1995, 613-541-5395.

#632
Joyceville Road/
Frontenac Road 16/
Joyceville

Joyceville Road connects to the north with Highway 15 to Ottawa and to the south with Highway 2 leading to Gananoque.

➤ SOUTH

Services:

Husky Service Centre, open 24 hours.

Off the Beaten Track: In a two-storey cedar log house in Grass Creek Park, wood is king. The MacLachlan Woodworking Museum celebrates "wood in the service of man" with displays and exhibits of traditional woodworking and the almost forgotten trades of the cooper and the blacksmith. The museum is located 4.5 kilometres from the 401, south on Joyceville Road and east on Highway 2. Open mid-May to Labour Day, daily 10 A.M. to 5 P.M.; March 1 to mid-May and Labour Day to

October 31, open Wednesday to Sunday noon to 4 P.M. Admission charge, 613-542-0543.

Picnic in the Park: Grass Creek Park, adjacent to the museum, spreads out to the river's edge with a beach area, picnic tables, barbecues, children's playground, washrooms and change rooms. This is not a wilderness park. No charge.

Special Events: At the Pittsburgh Township Sheep Dog Trials, held in Grass Creek Park on the weekend following the August Civic Holiday weekend, border collies and their trainers from across North America compete for top honours. Sheep shearing and wool spinning are demonstrated. Crafts and refreshments. Admission charge. Saturday and Sunday 8 A.M. to 6 P.M., 613-546-3283.

➤ NORTH

No services until Joyceville (population 60).

On the Road Again: Gananoque is 12 kilometres east on Highway 2.

#645
Highway 32/
Crosby/Gananoque

Gananoque (pronounced gannon-ock-way), south on Highway 32, is the gateway to the 1000 Islands

(Brockville to the east and Kingston to the west claim similar status). Many residents of the town of 5,200 live in century-old homes on tree-lined streets, and work in small businesses with longtime family connections. Donevan's Hardware on King Street, still operated by the Donevan family, has been in business since 1872. Another King Street business, R.J. Deir & Sons Ltd., has been selling fine British woollens since 1904; and the Townsend Division of Textron Canada Ltd. has produced rivets continually since 1869. Continuity in Gananoque is commonplace.

➣ SOUTH
Services:

The parking meters on King Street East in front of the post office are the best bargain in town. It costs only a penny to park here, for a maximum of 15 minutes. That's just enough time to pop into the post office to collect your mail. Don't put a nickel in—you'll still only get 15 minutes' parking.

Newspaper: *The Gananoque Reporter*, published weekly on Wednesdays.

Tourist Information: At the Gananoque and District Chamber of Commerce building on King Street,

right beside the Gananoque River, ask for the walking-tour brochure. Open year-round, July and August, daily 8 A.M. to 8 P.M.; September through June, daily 9 A.M. to 6 P.M. 1-800-561-1595.

To Market: On Saturday mornings mid-May through October, a farmers' market is held behind the Knights of Columbus building at the corner of Stone Street and Garden Street.

Factory Outlet: *Gan Shoe Outlet*, 180 King Street, for Naturalizer and Connie shoes and boots. Open Monday through Saturday 9:30 A.M.

Pitch Pines

The scraggly, tortured pines in the 1000 Islands area are rare pitch pines, able to survive here at the northern limit of their range because of the relatively mild climate of the islands and the acid soil of the Canadian Shield. A sign identifies a small stand of the trees beside the parkway just west of Brown's Bay Park. The old cones hanging on the branches are an easily recognizable feature of the species. The familiar silhouette of a contorted pine tree on a rough granite outcropping prompted the adoption of *Pinus rigida* as the symbol of the St. Lawrence Islands National Park. Pitch pines grow on many of the islands. The largest stand is in the park area on Hill Island.

to 5:30 P.M.; Friday till 8:30 P.M., 613-382-2633.

Go Wild: Wild Kingdom displays exotic and native animals in a 50-acre (20 ha) site just south of the 401 at 855 Stone Street North. Open May, June, September, daily 9 A.M. to 5 P.M.; July and August, daily 9 A.M. to 7 P.M. Picnic area and restaurant, 613-382-7141.

Take a Tour: The 1000 Islands are best seen by boat and spectacular in any season. Boat tours can be taken from Kingston, Gananoque, Ivy Lea, Rockport and Brockville. In Gananoque, tours depart from Water Street.

Picnic in the Park: Gananoque has a number of parks—along the Gananoque River in town and along the St. Lawrence River—but the one with the most atmosphere is Bluff Park. It is small, has few facilities and no water access, but from its high vantage point, the view of the river and the islands is magnificent. Follow King Street west through town, past the elaborately Victorian Victoria Rose Inn and turn left at Osborne and left again at Windsor Drive. No charge.

Off the Beaten Track: Get a bird's-eye view of the 1000 Islands. James Bay Helicopters Ltd., 700 King Street East, offers helicopter tours of the islands, May through October, daily 10 A.M. to sunset. The shortest tours are 10 minutes, 613-382-3700.

➤ **NORTH**

Services:

OPP: Just north of the 401, 613-382-2195.

On the Road Again: Drive through Gananoque on King Street East until it becomes Highway 2 and return to the 401 at IC #648 or take the scenic 1000 Islands Parkway along the river, past the small villages of Ivy Lea and Rockport.

INTERCHANGE

#647
1000 Islands Parkway

The 1000 Islands Parkway (IC #647) and Highway 2 (IC #648) exit together from the 401. The 1000 Islands Parkway extends only eastward from IC #647 to its eastern terminus at IC #685, west of Brockville.

The 40-kilometre route of the 1000 Islands Parkway along the craggy shoreline of the St. Lawrence River past the villages of Ivy Lea and Rockport offers tantalizing views of some of the approximately 1,800 islands. Although the traffic is steady in the peak summer months, the area is not overrun with commercial tourist attractions. Join the Parkway at any of the exits between IC #647 and IC #685 or return to the 401 at any of these interchanges. The bridges to the United States and Hill Island are accessible from the Parkway.

For services to the west on Highway 2, see IC #648. The Parkway replaces Highway 2 east.

Services: Motels and resorts, restaurants and gas stations are spread out along the Parkway. Boat tours operate from the villages of Ivy Lea and Rockport and have the advantage of beginning their tours in the thick of the islands. For specific information on interchanges between IC #647 and IC #685, check the service information for each interchange.

Picnic in the Park: At Grey's Bay Mini Park, very close to the western entrance of the Parkway, travellers can picnic and swim. No charge.

Take a Hike: Six kilometres from the 401, at Landon Bay Centre, nature trails, a scenic lookout, a swimming pool and interpretive programs are available from mid-May till mid-September. There is no swimming access to the St. Lawrence River. Admission charge. See IC #685 for more information on the 1000 Islands and the Parkway.

➤ EAST

Services: The 1000 Islands Parkway replaces Highway 2 east (see IC #648). There are no services directly east on County Road 2, north of the 401.

➤ WEST

Services:

 Burger King

  Esso

  DAYS INN The Best Value Under The Sun™

#648
Highway 2/Gananoque

Westbound travellers should exit here to reach Gananoque. Highway 2 west becomes King Street in downtown Gananoque.

#659
Reynolds Road/
Leeds/Grenville Road 3/
Landsdowne

Reynolds Road meets the 1000 Islands Parkway 2.5 kilometres to the south. Ivy Lea is 2 kilometres west on the Parkway.

To the north, County Road 3 leads to the village of Landsdowne (population 420).

➤ SOUTH

Services:

Tourist Information: On the northeast corner of Reynolds Road and the 1000 Islands Parkway, the Rideau Lakes and 1000 Islands Council operates a year-round tourist information centre. Open May through Labour Day, daily 8:30 A.M. to 6 P.M. Hours vary in the off-season months, 613-659-2191.

Take a Tour: Boat tours of the 1000 Islands depart from Ivy Lea mid-May to mid-October.

Boldt Castle

By the second half of the 19th century, life in the colonies was not all homespun woollens and handcarved utensils; the fortunes acquired through ingenuity, entrepreneurship and in some cases, even corruption, were flaunted with grandiose and excessive status symbols. Henry Pellatt's opulent Casa Loma and the Hearst castle in San Simeon were still to be constructed when George Boldt, millionaire hotelier, turned his attention to the current "in" vacation spot, the 1000 Islands. President Grant's week of fishing in 1872 at George Pullman's turreted summer home marked the beginning of a era of 1000 Islands popularity that would last until the First World War.

For their summer retreat, Boldt and his wife Louise chose Hart Island and set out in 1900 to build the quintessential Rhine castle Boldt remembered from his early, impoverished days in Europe. In a gesture surely affordable by only the very rich, Boldt proclaimed his undying love for Louise by reshaping the island to resemble a heart and by renaming it Heart Island. Two or three million dollars and 4 years later, construction was underway on 11 buildings and details on 120 castle rooms were being finalized when in January 1904, Louise died. All work on the castle ceased, and George Boldt never returned to the island.

Up until 1977, when the 1000 Island Bridge Authority acquired the property and undertook to restore and repair it, the castle had been neglected. In its refurbished and almost-completed state, Boldt Castle is a monument to a powerful love and to an era of incredible excesses.

Within the castle, exhibits relate the story of the Boldts and tell of turn-of-the-century island life, and local craftspeople display and sell their work. Admission charge. The castle is open to the public from late May to mid-October (boat access only, via private craft or boat tours), daily 10 A.M. to 6 P.M., 1-800-847-5263.

➤ NORTH
Services: At 2 kilometres

Fair Days: Lansdowne Fair, an agricultural fair held here since 1864, continues each year on the first weekend in August.

On the Road Again: Access Highway 137 and the bridge to the United States from the 1000 Islands Parkway east.

INTERCHANGE

#661
Highway 137/
Hill Island/
Bridge to USA

Highway 137 leads south only, to Hill Island, the 1000 Islands International Bridge and Interstate 81. The first three spans of the bridge connect the mainland to Hill Island, still on the Canadian side. Drive this far on the bridge for a sky-high view of the St. Lawrence and the islands. No passport is required; just pay a modest toll fee.

Prime Minister William Lyon MacKenzie King and President Franklin Delano Roosevelt opened the bridge in August 1938 as a co-operative effort of the two countries. The five spans of the bridge range in length from 4,500 feet (1370 m) to only 34 feet (10 m), and rise above the river anywhere from 15 feet (4.5 m) to 150 feet (45 m). In total, the bridge and its connector roads cover 13 kilometres.

➤ SOUTH
Services: On Hill Island

Tourist Information: An Ontario Travel Information Centre is open on Hill Island from mid-May till Thanksgiving, daily from 9 A.M. to 8 P.M. Washrooms.

Factory Outlets: On Hill Island: *Black & Decker Factory Outlet*, small appliances, outdoor products and electric tools. Open daily 9 A.M. to 5:30 P.M., 613-659-4034. *Rob McIntosh Warehouse Outlet*, china, crystal and gifts. Open daily 9:30 A.M. to 6 P.M., 613-659-2626. Hours vary seasonally.

Take a Tour: On a clear day, you can see for miles from the 400-foot-high (122 m) observation deck of the 1000 Islands Skydeck. High-speed elevators whisk visitors to the top. Open May to mid-June, Labour Day till mid-October, daily 9 A.M. to 6 P.M.; mid-June till Labour Day, daily 8 A.M. to 8 P.M. Admission charge, 613-659-2335.

On the Road Again: Boat tours of the 1000 Islands begin in the village of Rockport, a few kilometres east on the Parkway.

#675
Mallorytown Road/
Leeds/Grenville Road 5/
Mallorytown

Mallorytown Road leads north 1 kilometre to Mallorytown and south 2.3 kilometres to Mallorytown Landing.

➤ SOUTH
Services:

Picnic in the Park: North of the Parkway, in Mallorytown Landing, the administrative offices of the St. Lawrence Islands National Park share space in the park with a hiking trail and campsites. South of the Parkway, on the St. Lawrence River, there is a day-use area with swimming, picnicking, playground, washroom and boating facilities. The day-use area also includes a visitor centre and an exhibit of a gunboat wreck from the War of 1812, retrieved from nearby Brown's Bay. The park is accessible year-round but most facilities are open only from Victoria Day to Thanksgiving.

There is a parking charge when facilities are open. The rest of the St. Lawrence Islands National Park is composed of islands and parts of islands, accessible only by boat.

Step Back in Time: A small family graveyard, 3.5 kilometres west on the parkway, is a poignant reminder of the terribly difficult life of the early settlers. Parents William and Abigail La Rue are buried beside six of their nine children, who predeceased them. The oldest, Ann, was 17 years, 6 days at the time of her death; the youngest, Mary, only 1 month, 20 days when she died. The La Rue Mills Historic Cemetery is just beside the Parkway. Watch for the marker.

➤ NORTH
Services:

In Mallorytown, west on Highway 2

Roll Back the Clock: Industry has come and gone in Mallorytown, now a village of only 500 residents. The bricks used in the construction of the United Church and the three-storey brick Victorian house to the west on Highway 2 probably came from one of the four brickyards operating in the area in the mid-1800s. The Royal Ontario Museum in Toronto has in its collection a few pieces of early glass of a delicate aquamarine shade believed to have been produced at a glassworks just a mile away. Nearby, a short-lived and less-than-prosperous gold mine kindled gold fever for a few years in the 1870s.

On the Road Again: Continue east on the Parkway for Brown's Bay Park. See IC #685. For much of the way to Brockville, County Road 2 north of the 401 runs right alongside the freeway, but at a less frantic pace. Eastbound travellers in need of a break might prefer this route through farm country.

INTERCHANGE

#685
1000 Islands
Parkway

Interchange #685 is the westbound exit to the 1000 Islands Parkway. For the eastbound entrance to the Parkway, see IC #647. Join the Parkway at any of the exits between IC #685 and IC #647 or return to the 401 at any of these interchanges. The bridge to the United States and Hill Island are accessible from the Parkway.

Services: Check the interchanges between IC #685 and IC #647 for services available at those points. Although there are motels and resorts, restaurants, gas stations and boat tour companies along the route, the area is not spoiled by commercialization.

Picnic in the Park: Brown's Bay Park, 5 kilometres west on the Parkway, is the oldest of all the Parks of the St. Lawrence. In an idyllic setting on the shore of the

1000 Island Dressing

One day while cruising on his yacht in the 1000 Islands, George Boldt, owner of the Waldorf Astoria Hotel and builder of Boldt Castle, requested that his chef prepare a different dressing for his salad. From the limited supplies on board, Chef Oscar concocted a tangy mayonnaise dressing that Boldt later popularized in the Waldorf Astoria's dining room. He claimed that the bits of green in it represented the many islands of the St. Lawrence. Any all-purpose cookbook includes a recipe for 1000 Island dressing. This one comes from a 1967 community cookbook produced in Prescott as a Centennial project.

1 cup (250 mL) mayonnaise
1/2 cup (125 mL) chili sauce
3 hard-cooked eggs, chopped
1 1/2 dill pickles, chopped
1/3 cup (75 mL) chopped celery
1 green pepper, minced
1 small onion, minced
Combine and chill.

St. Lawrence River, the park's sandy beaches, trails, picnic facilities, food concession, washrooms and boat launch area attract day-use visitors. Open Victoria Day to Thanksgiving. Admission charge, 613-923-5087.

Off the Beaten Track: A little less than 2 kilometres west of Brown's Bay Park is Chimney Island, a small, craggy island with only a lone chimney. The most recent of a number of chimneys on the island, this chimney was rebuilt in this century. The story is told that the first chimney was built as early as 1799 or 1800 by a French Canadian and his part native Canadian bride. He was eventually found in his canoe by the water's edge with a tomahawk in his head. His bride was never found, and neither his identity nor the identity of his murderer were ever discovered.

INTERCHANGE

#687
Highway 2/Brockville

Highway 2 east, at this point a four-lane highway without controlled access, is the first of three exits into Brockville (population 21,000). It is a 7-kilometre drive to the city limits and another 2.5 kilometres to the courthouse square. Downtown Brockville can be reached faster from either IC #696 or IC #698. Highway 2 west disappears for a while. The roadway west and north of the 401 is County Road 2; the roadway west and south of the 401 is the 1000 Islands Parkway. Westbound travellers can pick up the 1000 Islands Parkway at the next interchange, IC #685.

➢ EAST
Services:

➢ WEST

There are no services on County Road 2 until Mallorytown.

On the Road Again: The drive into Brockville on Highway 2 makes a pleasant change of pace. For a view of the St. Lawrence River, try any of the sideroads or streets south. Return to the 401 at IC #696 or IC #698.

INTERCHANGE

#696
Highway 29/Brockville
★

Downtown Brockville is located 2 kilometres south of the 401. Highway 29 north of the 401 leads to Smiths Falls.

Brockville, a river city, was originally settled in 1784 by United Empire Loyalists. It flourished as Upper Canada prospered, and by the early 20th century it was known as a playground for the rich and famous.

➢ SOUTH
Services:

Brockville Centre (37 stores). Most services available in downtown Brockville.

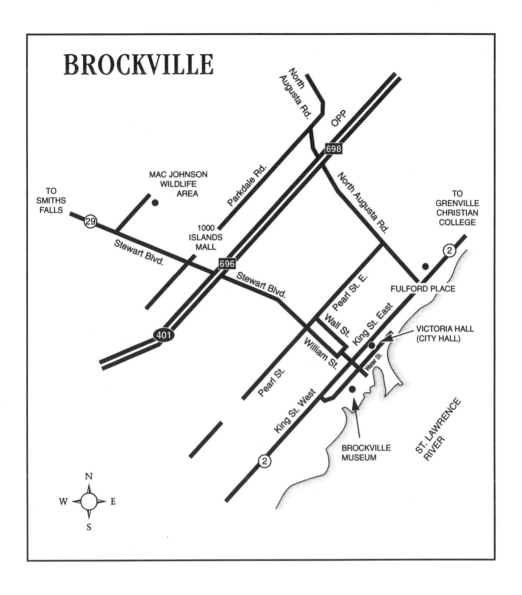

BROCKVILLE

Hospitals: Brockville General Hospital, Emma and Pearl Streets, 613-345-5645. St. Vincent de Paul Hospital, 42 Garden Street, 613-342-4461.

Newspaper: *The Recorder & Times*, published daily.

Radio Stations: CFJR AM 1450, CHXL FM 103.7

Tourist Information: Two summer tourist centres, one on Blockhouse Island at the foot of Market Street and the other, a kiosk on the west side of Highway 29, operate daily from 9 A.M. to 7 P.M. At Blockhouse Island, picnic facilities, washrooms and a snack bar are available. Information is also available at the Brockville Museum at 5 Henry Street, open Victoria Day to Thanksgiving daily, and limited hours off-season; and at the tall, square, Italianate Vitoria Hall (City Hall) on King Street, open Monday through Friday 8:30 A.M. to 4:30 P.M. (closed during the lunch hour), 613-342-8772.

Roll Back the Clock: The tale of Brockville's successful past is told in the architectural archives of the downtown streets. Take a walk and see the riverside mansions of King Street East, the New England-type town square anchored with a church on every corner, and the oldest railway tunnel in Canada. A publication, "Brockville's King Street East, A Walking Tour," can be purchased at the Brockville Museum or City Hall.

To Market: A farmers' market takes place Tuesday, Thursday and Saturday mornings on Market Street West from early May till late October.

Special Events: During Riverfest, the city celebrates summer with a full slate of concerts and entertainment events for the whole family. The event begins on a Friday, 10 days before the July 1st (Canada Day) weekend and continues until the Sunday of the Canada Day weekend.

Season's Best: From June through September and from November through February, the city's historical buildings, landmarks and trees come alive with 25,000 lights in the Symphony of Lights.

➤ NORTH

Services:

  Burger King HARVEY'S swiss chalet chicken + ribs McDonald's

Tim Hortons.

  Esso   PETRO-CANADA ®

 Comfort Inn

1000 Islands Mall (60-plus stores)

Pick a Peck: Freshly picked fruits and vegetables in season are available at Clows Country Market, 5 kilometres north on Highway 29. May to mid-October, Monday through Friday 9 A.M. to 8 P.M.; Saturday and Sunday 9 A.M. to 6 P.M., 613-345-1720.

Take a Hike: For the Mac Johnson Wildlife Area, continue north on Highway 29 for 4.5 kilometres. Turn east at the Fourth Concession Road and travel 2 more kilometres. The conservation area centres around a large reservoir used for boating (non-motorized) and fishing in the summer and skating and ice-sailing in the winter. Hiking and cross-country ski trails, picnic facilities, washrooms. No charge.

On the Road Again: King Street East in downtown Brockville leads directly to North Augusta Road (IC #698). Parkdale Road (just north of the 401), east of Highway 29, passes by the 1000 Islands Mall and meets North Augusta Road.

#698
North Augusta Road/
Brockville

North Augusta Road is the eastern-most exit to Brockville. For down-town Brockville, travel south on North Augusta Road 2.3 kilometres to King Street and turn west. See IC #696 for more Brockville information.

➤ SOUTH
Services:

Hospital: Brockville General Hospital, 75 Emma Street, 613-345-5645. For Brockville's second hospital, see IC #696.
Step Back in Time: Visit Fulford Place at 287 King Street East to appreciate the strength and success of George Fulford's formula for Dr. William's Pink Pills for Pale People. The impressive 20,000-square-foot stone mansion on the shore of the St. Lawrence River, complete with original furnishings, provides a glimpse into the lives of the wealthy at the turn of the century. The estate was used as a location site for the 1983 TV movie *Little Gloria Happy at Last.* Open Wednesday and weekends 1 P.M. to 5 P.M. Admission charge, 613-498-3003.
Bargain Hunt: At the River City Traders Flea Market, 1.5 kilometres

south of the 401 on North Augusta Road, home baking, crafts and other flea-market finds are for sale on Sunday from 9 A.M. to 5 P.M., 613-498-4894.

➤ NORTH

OPP: On Parkdale Road (continues north from North Augusta Road) less than 1 kilometre north, 613-345-1790.
On the Road Again: King Street East in Brockville becomes Highway 2 and passes a miniature golf course, antique shops, garden centres and motels on the way to Maitland, IC #705.

Grenville Christian College, 5 kilometres east of Brockville, hosts the Great Balloon Rodeo every year on the Father's Day weekend in June. Family activities begin on the Thursday evening and continue through Sunday. Weather permitting and only early in the day (usually between 5:30 and 7:30 A.M.) and/or in the evening (usually between 6:30 and 8:30 P.M.), balloons of all shapes and sizes take to the air. Watch from a distance or join the festivities on the spacious school grounds. Just remember, the balloons go up only at these times and then only when atmospheric conditions are favourable, 613-345-5521.

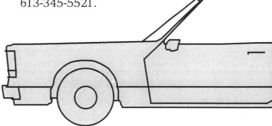

INTERCHANGE

#705
Maitland Road/ Leeds/Grenville Road 15/ Maitland/ Merrickville

Maitland Road leads south 2 kilometres to the village of Maitland and north eventually to Merrickville.

➤ SOUTH
Services:

Chip wagon (seasonal)

Roll Back the Clock: Maitland has mellowed more than modernised over the years. The French built ships at this site in the 18th century and Loyalists established a farming community here in the 19th century. However, Prescott, whose deep-water port served the fledgling country's increased river trade, and Brockville, site of the area courthouse and gaol from 1808, eventually surpassed Maitland in commercial successes. Maitland, overlooked in the 20th-century quest for new, bigger and better, remains a living museum.

There are no museums and no historic buildings open to the public, but you can see a lot just walking the streets. The Customs House Antique Shop may still have copies of "Maitland, 'A Very Neat Village Indeed.'"

Season's Best: In mid to late May, in the field just to the west of the old stone windmill, sheep and donkeys graze among clumps of daffodils. The farmhouse to the west, looking every bit the country manor, dates to 1861.

On the Road Again: Follow the St. Lawrence River along Highway 2 east, past Homewood, a Georgian stone house built in 1800 for Dr. Solomon Jones. He was an early Loyalist and the first and, for many years, only doctor between Cornwall and Gananoque. The property granted to Solomon Jones and his family as reward for their loyalty to the Crown during the American War of Independence remained in the Jones family for seven generations. Much of the memorabilia accumulated over those 172 years is on display. Homewood Museum is open April through November, Monday through Friday 10 A.M. to 4 P.M., and weekends in July and August. Small admission charge.

Farther along Highway 2 in a shady grove of trees overlooking the river, Barbara Heck, founder of Methodism in North America, is buried in the early cemetery beside the Blue Church. Return to the 401 by Edward Street in Prescott, IC #716.

➤ NORTH

A sign on Maitland Road: "IF YOU HAVE EATEN TODAY, THANK A FARMER."

#716
Edward Street/Prescott

Edward Street leads directly south 2 kilometres to downtown Prescott.

➤ SOUTH
Services:

 Burger King

More services in downtown Prescott on King Street.

OPP: On Edward Street opposite the eastbound exit from the 401, 613-925-4221.

Newspaper: *Prescott Journal*, weekly on Wednesday.

Tourist Information: Information on local attractions, including the Heritage Prescott walking-tour booklet, is available at the tourist information centre located in a mini lighthouse on the redeveloped waterfront at the foot of Edward Street. Open daily during July and August.

Roll Back the Clock: Prescott was first settled by United Empire Loyalists in 1784, and became an important link during the 19th century in the transportation of goods from Montreal to the developing settlements of Upper Canada. Considered vulnerable to attack from the Americans during the War of 1812, the town was fortified on the present site of Fort Wellington. Today the town's fine 19th-century homes attest to the wealth of its early citizens. In keeping with Prescott's image as "The Fort Town," its fire hydrants are painted to resemble toy soldiers.

To Market: A farmers' market takes place from May through October on Tuesday, Thursday and Saturday mornings in the parking lot by the clock on King Street.

Factory Outlets: These three outlets are located in the same general area. Look for the sign indicating a right turn immediately south of the railway overpass. *Hathaway Factory Outlet Store*, men's and women's shirts and sweaters, Clarendon Street, open Monday through Friday 9:30 A.M. to 4:30 P.M.; Saturday 9 A.M. to 4 P.M., 613-925-1530. *Portolano Outlet Centre*, men's and women's leather and wool gloves, scarves and hats, 840 Walker Street open Monday through Friday, 10 A.M. to 5 P.M.; Saturday 10 A.M. to 4 P.M., 613-925-4242. *Paderno Factory Store*, stainless steel cookware, St. Lawrence Street, in the 1851 train station. Open mid-May to mid-October, Monday through Saturday 10 A.M. to 6 P.M.; Sunday noon to 4 P.M. Winter hours vary, 613-925-0195.

Step Back in Time: Fort Wellington was built in 1838 on the site of fortifications dating to 1813. Interpretive staff in period costumes recount the fort's role in the defence of the St. Lawrence River during the troubles with the Americans in 1838. Located at King Street East and Van Koughnet Street. Open mid-May to September 30, daily 10 A.M. to 5 P.M.; October to mid-May by appointment, 613-925-2896. Admission charge.

Two museums in Prescott document different aspects of life in Upper Canada. The Forwarder's Museum on Water Street displays artefacts relating to Prescott's role in the transportation of goods up the St. Lawrence. Open mid-May to Labour Day, Monday through Saturday 10 A.M. to 4 P.M.; Sunday noon to 4 P.M. Donations accepted.

The Stockade Barracks and Hospital Museum at 356 East Street was built in 1810 to serve as a barracks during the War of 1812.

It was later used as a military hospital for Fort Wellington. Open weekends and holidays 10 A.M. to 5 P.M.

Picnic in the Park: Centennial Park is on the St. Lawrence River, south on Ann Street from King Street West. Picnic tables, washrooms, swimming pool and picnic beach. No charge.

Off the Beaten Track: Prescott's first settlers are buried in an early cemetery only a few hundred metres from the 401 on the west side of Edward Street. The Sandy Hill Cemetery, originally a Jessup family burial ground, was bequeathed to the town by the third Edward Jessup, grandson of Prescott's founder, Major Edward Jessup.

Purple Loosestrife

There's no denying that the summer swaths of magenta spikes are gorgeous, but purple loosestrife, an import from Europe in the early 1800s and a garden plant once revered as a hardy perennial, is now on most naturalists' hit lists. A single plant is capable of producing 2.7 million seeds, which need only the wind to carry them to a suitable germinating location—more often than not, a place where native vegetation is already established. Very quickly, loosestrife chokes out the native plants and covers the area. The "pushy" purple plant flourishes beside roadsides, in ditches and in wetlands with a remarkable persistence. Since herbicides cannot be used near water, and biological warfare is just beginning, the only solution, and one feasible only for small stands, is to physically remove each entire plant. If the tiniest piece of root, leaf or flower is left behind, the plant may regenerate.

Family members buried here, at the top of the steps, include Simeon Covell, whose headstone dates to 1798. The cemetery continues in use today.

Special Events: Loyalist Days take place from the second to third weekend in July. The Fort Wellington Military Pageant features artillery duels, military encampments and reenactments of the battle for control of the fort, and is the climax of the 10-day summer festival on the final weekend of the event.

➤ NORTH

On the Road Again: Follow Highway 2 east for 5 kilometres to Johnstown and return to the 401 via Highway 16. Windmill Point, described in IC #721, is between Prescott and Johnstown and can be accessed from either exit.

INTERCHANGE

#721
Highway 16/ Johnstown/Ottawa/ Kemptville/ Bridge to USA

Highway 16 leads north to Ottawa, and south to the International Bridge to the United States, the four-corner community of Johnstown, and the St. Lawrence River.

➤ SOUTH
Services: Highway 2 west

The Bridgeview Marina & Restaurant, a family-style restaurant west on Highway 2, is open early for breakfast every day, 6 A.M. to 9 P.M. 613-925-5663.

Tourist Information: An Ontario Travel Information Centre is located on the east side of Highway 16, 1 kilometre south of the 401. Open mid-May to Labour Day, daily 9 A.M. to 8 P.M.

Step Back in Time: At Windmill Point, about 3 kilometres west on Highway 2, cast-metal tablets document the 1838 Battle of the Windmill, in which Canadian rebels and American sympathizers fought against the local militia and British regulars. Sixty of the captured rebels were deported to Australia, eleven were hanged and the others freed. Watch carefully for the sign and turn left toward the river. Picnic area. No charge.

Season's Best: In mid to late May, old-fashioned purple and white lilacs bloom in profusion at Windmill Point.

➤ NORTH
Services:

Angelo's Restaurant/Truck Stop is open 7 days a week: Sunday to Thursday, 24 hours a day; Friday closed at 1 A.M.; Saturday open at 6 A.M., closed at midnight; Sunday open at 7 A.M., 613-925-5158.

On the Road Again: Drive east along the St. Lawrence River on Highway 2 to the next small community, Cardinal—past Grenville Park (camping and day use), North Channel Cemetery and the Johnstown Motel. Return to the 401 via Shanley Road, IC #730.

INTERCHANGE

730
Shanly Road/
Cardinal

The village of Cardinal (population 1,500) is 3 kilometres south on Shanley Road. Take Shanley Road north to hook up with Highway 16, which leads to Ottawa.

➤ **SOUTH**
Services:

730 Truck Stop open 24 hours, except closed Saturday 9 P.M. to Sunday 7 A.M. Gas bar 613-657-1128; truck stop 613-657-3155.

In Cardinal

Roll Back the Clock: Three times, men and machinery have attempted to beat the hazardous Galops Rapids of the St. Lawrence and in so doing have shaped Cardinal. The first canal was built around the outside of the village in 1844, in an attempt to beat the swift currents around Point Cardinal.

In 1901 a second canal was constructed through the peninsula. It transformed the village of Cardinal into an island community and necessitated a swing bridge to connect the point with the mainland. The weathered limestone-block walls are easily visible from Highway 2 east. With the completion of the St. Lawrence Seaway in the late 1950s, parts of the 1901 canal were filled in, the swing bridge was removed, and Point Cardinal once more became part of the mainland.

Picnic in the Park: From Shanley Road, cross Highway 2 and continue south down the hill to the water's edge. At the time of the construction of the St. Lawrence Seaway, the local Canadian Legion branch acquired the major remaining section of land around the original canal and on it created Memorial Park and a new Legion Hall. This is a great spot for a picnic, right on the river bank. No charge. Picnic tables, washroom. Point Cardinal Marina.

➤ NORTH

On the Road Again: Highway 2 east from Cardinal to Iroquois follows the shore of the St. Lawrence. The plain stone farmhouses served the needs of early settlers.

INTERCHANGE

#738
Carman Road/
Iroquois

Carman Road leads south to Iroquois (2 kilometres).

➤ SOUTH
Services: East on Highway 2

Iroquois Mall (20 stores)

Baldi's Deli, in the mall, is not just potato salad and pastrami. Light meals, from hearty breakfasts to early dinners, are served Monday through Thursday 7 A.M. to 5 P.M.; Friday, 7 A.M. to 8 P.M.; Saturday 7 A.M. to 3 P.M.; Sunday 10 A.M. to 3 P.M. 613-652-1613.

Tourist Information: On Carman Road south of Highway 2, next to the campground, the town of Iroquois operates a tourist information kiosk during July and August.

Roll Back the Clock: In expectation of extensive flooding with the completion of the St. Lawrence Seaway and Power Project in 1958, the entire town of Iroquois, a Loyalist village settled in 1784, was relocated 1 kilometre north. Giant housemovers moved 150 houses. All other homes were lost and their owners were given financial compensation to rebuild. The village today is a combination of relocated century-old homes and 1950s bungalows. In the name of shipping progress, some villages of the St. Lawrence were totally lost, others were partially moved, but only Iroquois was completely recreated.

Tour the World: From the Seaway Lock Lookout you can watch ocean-going ships from around the world pass through the Iroquois locks. A chalkboard outside the snack bar lists the ships due, their nationality and their expected time of arrival. Picnic tables, washrooms. No charge. The pioneer cemetery to the north of the lock-viewing area contains interesting old tombstones.

Step Back in Time: Carman House, an 1820 riverside stone house next to the tourist information kiosk, is one of only three Iroquois homes not moved during the relocation of the town. It operates as a local museum in July and August, daily 10 A.M. to 4 P.M. Donations accepted.

Picnic in the Park: The Iroquois waterfront is one huge park with acres of green, beaches and picnic facilities. Continue south past the mall to the park.

➢ **NORTH**

On the Road Again: Follow the twists and turns of Highway 2 for 3 kilometres east to Lakeshore Drive and turn right. Drive along the water's edge past waterfront farms, apple orchards, Loyalist Park and Mariatown to Morrisburg. Before the completion of the canal in Morrisburg in 1847, Mariatown was the area's main settlement. Impressive waterfront mansions with slate mansard roofs, pillared porches, and three-storey towers line Lakeshore Drive and the surrounding streets of Morrisburg. Return to the 401 via IC #750.

Big Reds

It is not remarkable that John McIntosh, a United Empire Loyalist who arrived in the St. Lawrence area from New York in 1796, discovered a number of wild apple trees while clearing some of his property in 1811. The amazing thing is that now, almost 200 years later, the descendants of the big red apples from one of those trees are still popular around the world. Unlike the Sweet Winesap or the Yellow Transparent, the McIntosh apple has not slipped into obscurity. Instead, because Macs travel well, winter well and look and taste great, they have been perfect for large-scale marketing in the 20th century. Every McIntosh apple in the world can be traced to the apple tree on John McIntosh's farm.

A plaque in the village of Dundela, northeast of Iroquois (IC #738), marks the spot where the original tree grew until 1906. Just down the road at Smyth's Orchards, McIntosh apples are still harvested from trees grafted before the turn of the century. Macs and less familiar varieties such as Snows, Tolman Sweets and Bancrofts are for sale at Smyth's. Open daily August to April 9 A.M. to 5 P.M., 613-652-2477.

INTERCHANGE

#750
Highway 31/
Morrisburg/
Winchester

Highway 31 leads directly north past the town of Winchester to Ottawa (70 kilometres) and south 2 kilometres to Morrisburg, another one of the St. Lawrence communities originally settled by United Empire Loyalists after the American War of Independence in 1776.

Only one-third of the town of Morrisburg was moved to accommodate the St. Lawrence Seaway. Check the streets in the eastern part of town—Farlinger Avenue and Park Avenue are good places to start. Any house that looks older than the mid-1950s was probably moved to its present location. Don't miss the houses on Lakeshore Drive that were not moved.

➤ SOUTH
Services:

Village Plaza

OPP: On Highway 31, 613-543-2949.

Newspaper: *The Leader*, weekly on Wednesday.

Tourist Information: The town operates a seasonal tourist information centre in the parking lot of the Village Plaza. Open June to the end of September, 9 A.M. to 6 P.M.; later hours on weekends.

To Market: A small farmers' market operates every day in the Village Plaza parking lot from June through September. There is also a larger market on summer Saturday mornings on Highway 2 west beside the Upper Canada Playhouse.

Bookstore: At the Old Author's Farm, wall-to-wall and floor-to-ceiling shelves spill over with rare books, old books and even a few brand-new books. Ask for *Bowering's Guide to Eastern Ontario*, a recent publication that contains all you need to know about the area from Iroquois to the Quebec border. For this bookstore, follow Highway 31 south to Gibson Lane. Open May through October, daily 10 A.M. to 6 P.M. or by appointment, 613-543-3337.

Picnic in the Park: Continue south on Lakeshore Road to Riverside Park. Swimming. Picnic facilities. Washrooms.

Off the Beaten Track: Tucked into a private backyard at 17 Casselman Road, The Garden is open to visitors. With the use of recycled materials and with some financial support from local businesses, an ordinary backyard has been transformed into a showplace. Take Laurier Drive south from Highway 2, and turn left on Kyle Drive and then turn right on Casselman

Road. Just open the garden gate and feast your eyes. Seasonal. No charge.

➤ NORTH

Services:

Bargain Hunt: McHaffie's Flea Market, 3 kilometres north on Highway 31, is open year-round on Sunday from 9 A.M. to 4:30 P.M., 613-543-9000.

Off the Beaten Track: Every day from 1928 to 1942, thousands of people crowded into the hamlet of Williamsburg (population today 550). They all came to see Dr. Mahlon W. Locke, considered by some to be a miracle worker and by others, a quack. Dr. Locke believed that fallen arches were the cause of many ailments, including arthritis, and he treated the suffering and the twisted by manually manipulating their feet. In good weather the treatments were held on the lawn of his big white house and office in Williamsburg, 7 kilometres north of Morrisburg, just east of Highway 31 on County Road 18. Each treatment cost $1.00.

Residents rented out their bedrooms and slept in the woodshed. Twenty-three restaurants tried to feed the crowds. A luxury liner, the *Rapids Queen*, anchored off Morrisburg to take the overflow from the local hotels.

Rest your own feet at the Village Antiques & Tea Room in Williamsburg before returning to the 401. Open for lunch, high tea and dinner,

Wednesday through Sunday, 613-535-2463.

On the Road Again: If you have travelled north to Williamsburg, follow County Road 18 east about 20 kilometres through prosperous farm country to the sleepy hamlet of Osnabruck Centre and return to the 401 at IC #770. From Highway 2 east of Morrisburg, IC #758, Upper Canada Road is 8 kilometres away.

#758
Upper Canada Road/ Stormont/Dundas and Glengarry Road 41

Eastbound, take Upper Canada Road for Upper Canada Village and the Upper Canada Migratory Bird Sanctuary. Westbound, if you are planning to visit the Upper Canada Migratory Bird Sanctuary, exit at IC #770 and travel west on Highway 2 to the signs for the sanctuary on the left.

➤ SOUTH

Services: At Highway 2, 2 kilometres

As Large as Life: Dinosaur World is on Upper Canada Road, just a kilometre off the 401. The sculpted creatures are awesome. Open late May through September, daily 10 A.M. to 4 P.M. Admission charge, 613-543-2503.

Step Back in Time: Upper Canada Village was created to preserve the artefacts and buildings that would otherwise have been lost when the shores of the St. Lawrence River were flooded on July 1, 1958, to create Lake St. Lawrence. A visit here takes you back to a rural community of the 1860s; leave lots of time to tour the village. It is located east on Highway 2 about 4.5 kilometres from the 401. Open early May to Thanksgiving, daily 9:30 A.M. to 5 P.M. Call for winter hours, 613-543-3704. Admission charge.

The Queen Elizabeth Gardens, the Upper Canada Railroad, the Battle of Crysler's Farm Visitor Centre, and the Pioneer Memorial are adjacent to Upper Canada Village. The Upper Canada Golf Course is on the north side of Highway 2.

Picnic in the Park: The Crysler Beach Picnic Area, located just to the west of Upper Canada Village, offers a picnic area, sandy beach and children's playground. Washrooms. Open mid-May to Labour Day. No charge.

For the Birds: The Upper Canada Migratory Bird Sanctuary is the best goose pasture around. You can see countless bird species from the network of nature trails, but the Canada geese outnumber all others.

Forty-five hundred make their home in the area and another 10,000 stop here on their way south. From the middle of September to the end of October, park staff spread out corn each day at 2:30 P.M. The honking of the arriving flocks—on an average October day 1,500 to 3,000 birds—is deafening. The sanctuary is located 4 kilometres east of Upper Canada Village on Highway 2. It is 2.5 kilometres farther on Aultsville Road to the visitor centre and feeding station, but well worth the visit, particularly at feeding time. Visitor centre. Picnic facilities. Washrooms. No charge. 613-543-2024.

Off the Beaten Track: The road leading into the Upper Canada Bird Sanctuary, Aultsville Road, originally led to the village of Aultsville, one of the early Loyalist villages lost in the construction of the Seaway. Follow the road about 1 kilometre south to a checkerboard sign indicating a left bend in the road. Don't follow the bend. Instead, continue straight ahead to a small parking area and a barrier. Walk as far south as possible. At the water's edge the former village sidewalks break up and disappear beneath the water. See IC #778 for the Lost Villages Museum.

➢ NORTH

On the Road Again: Continue on Highway 2 east to Ingleside from the Upper Canada Migratory Bird Sanctuary and return to the 401 at IC #770.

#770
Dickinson Road/ Stormont/Dundas and Glengarry Road 14/ Ingleside

Dickinson Road leads south, 1.5 kilometres to Ingleside.

In case you're feeling lost, a marker on Dickinson Road south of the 401 announces your position on the 45th parallel: YOU ARE NOW HALFWAY TO THE EQUATOR. When you're travelling north on Dickinson Road, the sign reads: YOU ARE NOW HALFWAY TO THE NORTH POLE.

➤ **SOUTH**
Services:

West on Highway 2

Holstein Cattle

Although they are such a familiar sight that we never give them a second thought, the black-and-white cows grazing in farm fields are relative newcomers to Canada. In 1881, Michael Cook, a farmer in Eastern Ontario near the lost village of Aultsville (see IC #758), imported the first Holstein-Friesian cattle into Canada from stock raised by an American breeder. Descendants of the two bulls and ten cows that Cook imported have, for years, been the leading dairy producers in the province. This breed, long recognized in its native Holland for exemplary milk production, was prized by early Canadian farmers searching for a super dairy cow, capable of producing large quantities of milk and adaptable to long winters. Modern techniques of artificial insemination and embryo transplants have continued to improve the breed. The name Holstein-Friesian acknowledges the breed's origins in Holstein, a duchy of Prussia, and Friesland, a province in the Netherlands.

To see a life-size statue of a very great lady, exit at IC #232 in Woodstock. Springbank Snow Countess's lifetime butterfat production earned her world-champion status.

Roll Back the Clock: The construction of the St. Lawrence Seaway tamed the Long Sault (pronounced Soo) Rapids, reshaped the river's shoreline, and irrevocably changed the lives of those on "The Front." Caught in the path of progress, the hamlets of Aultsville, Farran's Point, Wales, Dickinson's Landing, Moulinette and Mille Roches, considered too small and too costly to relocate, were allowed to slip below the flooding waters. Two new towns, Ingleside and Long Sault, were created to replace them.

Long Sault Parkway: The eastern entrance to Long Sault Parkway is just east of Ingleside on Highway 2. By bridges and causeways, the 11-kilometre parkway connects twelve of the islands created by the flooding of the St. Lawrence River and then returns to the mainland at Long Sault. Day and overnight use. Picnic facilities, washrooms, beaches, fishing. Open May to late September. Admission charge.

➤ NORTH

On the Road Again: On Highway 2 east, watch for the Union Cemetery. The island directly in front of it was once part of the lost village of Wales. The Village Flea Market, 1 kilometre west of Long Sault, is open every day 10 A.M. to 5 P.M. except Monday. Watkins products are sold here.

INTERCHANGE

#778
Moulinette Road/ Stormont/Dundas and Glengarry Road 35/ Long Sault

Moulinette Road leads south 2.5 kilometres to Long Sault. The name Long Sault will always be a reminder of the Long Sault Rapids, once a 1.6-kilometre stretch of rough and treacherous water with a reputation for testing all river craft. The eastern entrance to the Long Sault Parkway is at Highway 2 and Moulinette Road.

➤ SOUTH

Services: At Highway 2

The River Front Diner, located, as its name suggests, beside the river, is a good place to find an early breakfast. Open daily from 6:30 A.M. till 8 P.M. or 9:00 P.M. Casual. Indoor and outdoor tables. Located east on Highway 2, next door to the Long Sault Marina, 613-534-8466.

OPP: To the east on Highway 2, 613-534-2223.

Step Back in Time: The Lost Villages Museum is located in a tiny 1840 log cabin 1.5 kilometres east of Long Sault on Highway 2 in Ault Park. Seven villages and 20,000 acres (8,100 ha) of farmland were lost to the rising waters of the St. Lawrence River. Open July and August, daily 9 A.M. to 4 P.M. No charge.

➢ NORTH

On the Road Again: Highway 2 east crosses Power Dam Road (IC #786) but access to the 401 east is not direct from Power Dam Road. The 401 west is accessible at IC #786. Picnic facilities and washrooms are available at Guidon Park, halfway between Long Sault and Cornwall on Highway 2 east.

INTERCHANGE

#786
Power Dam Road/ Stormont/Dundas and Glengarry Road 33

Power Dam Road exits only south from only the eastbound 401. It crosses Highway 2 on its way to the R.H. Saunders Generating Station. There is no exit from the westbound 401.

➢ SOUTH

Services: At Highway 2

On the Road Again: If you want to bypass Cornwall, do not leave the 401 at this exit. The first return to the 401 east is at IC #789. Highway 2 east leads to downtown Cornwall.

INTERCHANGE

#789
Highway 138/ Brookdale Avenue/ Cornwall
★

Highway 138 runs north 7 kilometres to the heritage village of St. Andrews. Brookdale Avenue is the most westerly of the three exits to Cornwall. It leads to the Seaway International Bridge and Massena, New York, and is Cornwall's service street, with many motels, gas stations, restaurants and fast food outlets. Downtown Cornwall is about 5 kilometres from the 401 (see IC #792 and IC #796 for more Cornwall information).

➢ SOUTH

Services: On Brookdale Avenue

Burger King

 Travelodge **RAMADA**

Brookdale Mall (40-plus stores)

More motels, gas stations and restaurants can be found on Vincent Massey Drive (becomes Highway 2 west) and in downtown Cornwall.

Tourist Information: The Ontario Travel Information Centre on Brookdale Avenue across from the Brookdale Mall is open year-round, mid-May to Labour Day daily 8 A.M. to 8 P.M.; off-season, daily 8:30 A.M. to 4:30 P.M. The Cornwall Regional Visitor and Convention Bureau at 1302 Second Street West is open year-round Monday through Friday 8:30 A.M. to 4:30 P.M., 1-800-937-4748. Ask for the "Le Village Historic Walking Tour" and the "Downtown Historic Walking Tour" brochures.

Step Back in Time: The United Counties Museum is located in Wood House at 731 Second Street West, just west of Brookdale Avenue. Built of limestone in 1840, it is a typical centre-hall Ontario farmhouse. As well as displaying a collection of local Canadiana, the museum offers slide presentations on local history, particularly on the Seaway and Sir John Johnson, founder of Cornwall. Open April to November, Tuesday through Saturday 11 A.M. to 5 P.M.; Sunday 2 P.M. to 5 P.M. No charge, 613-932-2381.

➤ NORTH

Services:

Antiques: Johnson's Antiques, north 3 kilometres on Highway 138, tempts the antique browser with thousands of items, from furniture to frames to fine glass. Open year-round, 7 days a week, 9 A.M. to 5 P.M., 613-932-0766 or 938-3358.

Off the Beaten Track: In St. Andrews West, a village 3.5 kilometres beyond Johnson Antiques, the old stone structures of the late 18th and early 19th centuries have withstood the test of time. The Catholic Parish Hall, built as a church between 1798 and 1801 by Gaelic-speaking, Highland Scots, is one of Ontario's oldest stone structures. In the pioneer cemetery across the road, MacDonalds, McDonalds and McDonnells attest to the Scottish beginnings of the area. The explorer Simon Fraser is buried here, as is John Sandfield Macdonald, prime minister of the Province of Canada from 1862 to 1864 and the first premier of Ontario.

Once a convent school, the Raisin River Heritage Centre, just a few hundred metres west on County Road 18, is now a museum. Open Sunday 2 to 4 P.M. No charge, 613-933-4072. The Cornwall Township Historical Society's brochure "Historical Sites of Cornwall Township" provides information on the St. Andrews heritage buildings and sites.

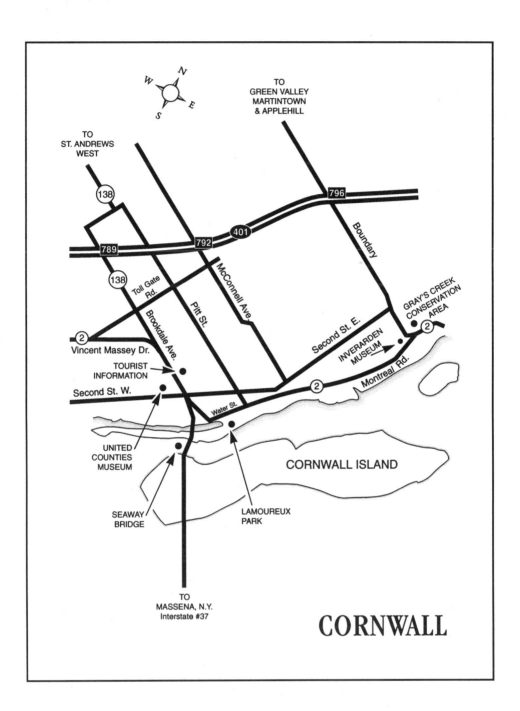

CORNWALL

On the Road Again: Follow Highway 2 east, now Montreal Road, to either McConnell Avenue or Boundary Road to return to the 401.

INTERCHANGE

#792
McConnell Avenue/
Cornwall

McConnell Avenue leads south into downtown Cornwall. To the north, rural Ontario takes over.

Cornwall (population 47,000), the eastern anchor of the Seaway Valley, is Ontario's most easterly city. It was settled in 1784 by Loyalists from New York State and Pennsylvania. In the mid-1800s, the city's character became more cosmopolitan with the influx of Francophones to work in the textile mills. In one of these cotton mills in 1882, Thomas Edison installed the first commercial electric-light system in North America. Today, the city is bilingual and the pulp and paper mill of Domtar Fine Papers is a mainstay of the economy.

➤ **SOUTH**

Services:

Fifth Wheel Truck Stop, open 24 hours.

Hospitals: Hotel Dieu Hospital, 840 McConnell Avenue, 613-938-4240; Cornwall General Hospital, 510 Second Street East, 613-932-3300.

Newspaper: *Standard Freeholder*, daily except Sunday.

Radio Stations: CJSS AM 1220, CFLG FM 104.5 (English), CHOD FM 92.1 (French), Akwasasne CKON FM 97.3

Tourist Information: The Cornwall Chamber of Commerce operates a tourist information centre in Lamoureux Park near the Cornwall Civic Complex, July and August, daily 10 A.M. to 7 P.M.

To Market: A farmers' market takes place Wednesday and Saturday mornings from mid-June through October on Third Street West in the municipal parking lot.

Special Events: Worldfest/ Festimonde, an international festival of song and dance, attracts participants from several countries for 6 days of concerts, dancing and displays. The event takes place each year in the week after Canada Day (July 1) at sites in Cornwall, 613-936-2222.

Picnic in the Park: Lamoureux Park's green acres spread out along the St. Lawrence River in Cornwall's revitalized downtown waterfront.

➤ NORTH

On the Road Again: Follow Montreal Road (Highway 2) east to Boundary Road IC #796 to return to the 401.

INTERCHANGE

#796
Boundary Road/
Cornwall

Boundary Road is the most easterly of the three exits to Cornwall. Turn west at Second Avenue or Montreal Road to reach downtown Cornwall. Montreal Road runs through the heart of Le Village, an area of the city in which the French-Canadian labour force lived in company housing close to the early textile factories. Inquire at the tourist information centres for the brochure "Le Village Historic Walking Tour." See IC #792 and IC #789 for more information on Cornwall.

To the north, township roads lead through the heart of rural Glengarry County.

➤ SOUTH
Services:

Take a Hike: Gray's Creek Conservation Area and Marina Complex is located about 3 kilometres south of the 401, east off Boundary Road.

Picnic facilities, nature trails. Washrooms and drinking water in the marina building.

Step Back in Time: Inverarden is a fine Regency cottage built in 1816 for a North West Company fur-trade partner, John McDonald. The house at 3332 Montreal Road (just west of Boundary Road), restored and furnished to circa 1825, is now a museum. Open April to November, Tuesday through Saturday 11 A.M. to 5 P.M.; Sunday 2 P.M. to 5 P.M. No charge, 613-938-9585.

➤ NORTH

On the Road Again: Follow Highway 2 east 8 kilometres to Summerstown and IC #804.

INTERCHANGE

#804
Summerstown Road/
Stormont/Dundas and
Glengarry Road 27/
Summerstown

Summerstown Station to the north of the 401 is not much more than a crossroads. Summerstown, 4 kilometres south, is a small riverside community.

➤ SOUTH
Services:

To the east on Highway 2, the Edgewater and the Glendale Restaurants offer dining on the shore of Lake St. Francis.

Off the Beaten Track: To the west of Summerstown on Highway 2, a historic marker at the side of the road tells the story of Fairfield, the imposing Italianate home at the end of the driveway. Cariboo Cameron used the considerable wealth he had acquired in British Columbia's goldfields to build this house in 1865 at a reputed cost of $20,000. Unfortunately, Cameron's beloved wife, Sophie, had died in British Columbia before the gold strike. To keep his promise to bring her body home, Cameron shipped her corpse in a metal, alcohol-filled casket 8,600 miles (13,850 km) by sea via the Isthmus of Panama. Sophie is buried in the graveyard of the Salem United Church, 0.6 km farther west on Highway 2.

➤ NORTH
Services:

Note the old, weathered and worn cowboy boots decorating the posts of the rail fence next-door to the gas station.

On the Road Again: To the east, Highway 2 toward Lancaster follows the shoreline of Lake St. Francis past Cameron's Point Campsite and Water Slide, a grazing herd of buffalo, Charlie's Go Kart & Miniature Golf, the Cooper Creek Conservation Area (see IC #814) and the Lancaster Inn.

#814
Highways 2 & 34/
Lancaster/
South Lancaster

Lancaster is immediately north of the 401 on Highway 34. Lancaster offers craft and speciality stores, as well as chip wagons and tea shops. Do not leave without sampling Lancaster perch either in a fish roll or as a plate dinner. The accompanying fish sauce is considered by some to be an acquired taste.

To the south, Highway 2 begins a journey across Ontario, paralleling the early water route along the St. Lawrence River and Lake Ontario. South Lancaster was the site of a 1784 settlement of Loyalists known as the Falkner Settlement.

➤ SOUTH
Services:

Roll Back the Clock: In South Lancaster, heed the warning at St. Andrew's Presbyterian Church: "Anyone parking here must preach the sermon." Turn left on Church Street to catch the humour of the current Reverend. The limestone church dates only to 1855 but replaces a earlier wooden church built in 1787. Walk south toward the waterfront to the resting place of early pioneers of the Falkner Settlement. In a cemetery enclosed by a low stone wall, century-old headstones give some perspective to the past.

Factory Outlet: The Rob McIntosh Warehouse Outlet is no ordinary outlet store. Out of a collection of old buildings (some moved to the site from other locations) china, kitchen and glass ware are offered at discount prices. Open Monday through Saturday 9:30 A.M. to 6 P.M.; Sunday 11 A.M. to 5 P.M., 613-347-2461.

Gifts Galore: In Auld Kirktown, just south of the 401, shop for local crafts and gifts. For hours, call 613-347-3527.

Off the Beaten Track: Walk south on King Street in South Lancaster past the boathouses to the end of the fishing pier. Look west. A conical stone cairn dominates a small island. To keep the idle Glengarry militiamen occupied during the winter after their 1838 tours of duty, Lieutenant-Colonel Lewis Carmichael set them to work building a cairn to honour Sir John Colborne, a former lieutenant-governor of Upper Canada and a military hero. The cairn is said to be 52 feet wide at its base and 52 feet high to acknowledge Sir John's successes in the Peninsular War as commander of the 52nd regiment. Boat access only. Binoculars help to see the cairn from the pier.

Take a Hike: At Cooper Marsh Conservation Area, 3 kilometres

Roadside Supermarket

Did you know that a supermarket grows in many of the ditches and marshes along the highway? At some time in the year, all parts of the cattail, except the leaves, are edible.

Start at the top. Early in the season, before the familiar sausage-like heads turn tawny with pollen, the immature flower spikes can be harvested, removed from their papery sheaths, boiled and eaten like corn on the cob. Once the flower ages, the golden-yellow pollen can be shaken and collected from the spikes and used as a flour extender in pancakes, breads and puddings. Natives used the dried and ground underground stems as another source of flour. The young shoots, if picked in the spring just as they emerge, are reported to taste like cucumber. Although I can't confirm any of these taste comparisons or preparation procedures, I am tempted to check out Cossack asparagus. Until the plants are close to a yard high, the young stems can be harvested, their outer rinds peeled, and the tender white insides eaten raw as a salad vegetable or cooked and served much like asparagus. Why has no one cultivated and marketed this incredible plant?

west on Highway 2, boardwalks, viewing platforms and hiking trails introduce visitors to a wetland environment. Picnic facilities. Visitor centre. Washrooms. Open year-round. No charge.

➤ **NORTH**
Services:

OPP: In Lancaster, turn left off Military Road/Highway 34 to Pine Street, 613-347-2449.

Off the Beaten Track: Turn west on Pine Street in Lancaster and follow County Road 17, 7 kilometres to Williamstown, a Scots town where many fur traders of the North West Company chose to retire. The town has many heritage buildings, and some are open to the public: St. Andrew's United Church, built in 1812, and its adjacent burial ground; the Bethune–Thompson House whose original kitchen is believed to date from the 1780s, open Sunday 1 P.M. to 5 P.M.; the Nor'Westers and Loyalist Museum, open Victoria Day through Labour Day, daily 1 P.M. to 5 P.M., Saturday and holidays 10 A.M. to 5 P.M., Labour Day to Thanksgiving, weekends only.

Rest awhile at Jack Delaney's Restaurant and Pub overlooking the Raisin River before continuing on.

Fair Days: Ontario's oldest fair, first held in 1808, takes place the second weekend in August each year in Williamstown.

On the Road Again: From Lancaster, follow County Road 17 east to Bainsville. Sangster's & Sons General Store/Post Office/Gas Station has it all. Return to the 401 at IC #825.

INTERCHANGE

#825
Curry Hill Road

Curry Hill Road is either your first or your last exit on Main Street, Ontario.

➤ **SOUTH**
Services:

➤ **NORTH**
Services:

On the Road Again: Suddenly it is over. With nary a sign, the 401 ends about 3 kilometres east of Curry Hill Road. One minute you are in Ontario, the next you are in Quebec. Bon voyage or bienvenue, whichever the case may be.

Metropolitan Toronto Interchanges

IC #	Interchange	
348	Renforth Drive	Exits eastbound only
350	Eglinton Avenue	Exits eastbound only
351	Carlingview Drive	Exits westbound only
352	Highway 427	Exits south to QEW
354	Dixon Road/Martin Grove Road	Alternate exit to airport
355	Belfield Road/Highway 409/ Highway 427 North	Exits westbound only/ Highway 409 to airport
356	Islington Avenue	
357	Weston Road	
359	Highway 400/Black Creek Drive	Highway 400 north to Barrie
362	Keele Street	
364	Dufferin Street	Exits eastbound only/Exit westbound via Allen Road
365	Allen Road	See page 73
366	Bathurst Street	Exits westbound only
367	Avenue Road	Highway 11A to downtown Toronto
369	Highway 11/Yonge Street	Toronto's east/west divider
371	Bayview Avenue	
373	Leslie Street	See page 73
375	Highway 404/Don Valley Parkway	Highway 404, north to Stouffville Don Valley Parkway, an expressway to downtown (extremely busy south-bound in morning rush hour and northbound in afternoon rush hour)
376	Victoria Park Avenue	
378	Warden Avenue	
379	Kennedy Road	
381	McCowan Road	
383	Highway 48/Markham Road	Highway 48 north to Markham
385	Neilson Road	
387	Morningside Avenue	

Guide to Highway Service Centre Locations

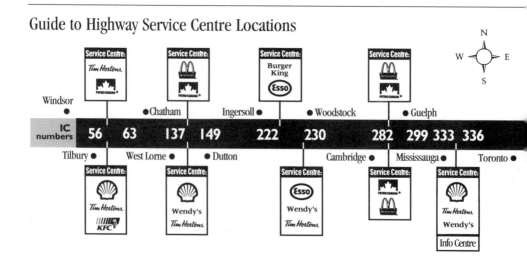

401 Interchanges

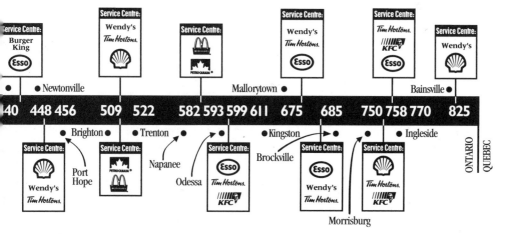